PIRACY IN
SOUTHEAST ASIA

IIAS/ISEAS Series on Maritime Issues and Piracy in Asia

Series Advisory Board

The **IIAS/ISEAS Series on Maritime Issues and Piracy in Asia** is an initiative to catalyse research on the topic of piracy and robbery in the Asian seas. Considerable attention in the popular media has been directed to maritime piracy in recent years reflecting the fact/perception that piracy is again a growing concern for coastal nations of the world. The epicentre of global pirate activity is the congested sea-lanes of Southeast Asia but attacks have been registered in wide-scattered regions of the world.

The **International Institute for Asian Studies** (IIAS) is a post-doctoral research centre based in Leiden and Amsterdam, the Netherlands. IIAS' main objective is to encourage Asian studies in the humanities and social sciences — and their interaction with other sciences — by promoting national and international co-operation in these fields. IIAS publications reflect the broad scope of the Institute's interests.

The **Institute of Southeast Asian Studies** (ISEAS) was established in Singapore as an autonomous organization in 1968. It is a regional centre dedicated to the study of socio-political, security and economic trends and developments in Southeast Asia and its wider geostrategic and economic environment. ISEAS Publications has issued over 2,000 scholarly books and journals since 1972.

IIAS/ISEAS Series on
Maritime Issues and Piracy in Asia

PIRACY IN SOUTHEAST ASIA
Status, Issues, and Responses

Edited by
Derek Johnson and Mark Valencia

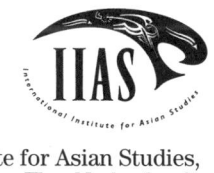

International Institute for Asian Studies,
The Netherlands

Institute of Southeast Asian Studies,
Singapore

First published in Singapore in 2005 by
ISEAS Publications
Institute of Southeast Asian Studies
30 Heng Mui Keng Terrace
Pasir Panjang
Singapore 119614

E-mail: publish@iseas.edu.sg
Website: http://bookshop.iseas.edu.sg

The responsibility for facts and opinions in this publication rests exclusively with the authors and their interpretations do not necessarily reflect the views or the policy of the publishers or their supporters.

ISEAS Library Cataloguing-in-Publication Data

Piracy in Southeast Asia: status, issues and responses / edited by Derek Johnson
and Mark J. Valencia.
1. Pirates—Asia, Southeastern.
2. Terrorism—Asia, Southeastern.
3. National security—Asia, Southeastern.
4. Naval strategy.
5. Sea control—International cooperation.
6. Sea-power—Asia, Southeastern.
I.   Johnson, Derek.
II. Valencia, Mark J.
DS526.7 P66   2005

ISBN 981-230-276-X (soft cover)
ISBN 981-230-326-X (hard cover)

Cover photo: Courtesy of Michael S. Yamashita, National Geographic Image Collection.

Typeset by Superskill Graphics Pte Ltd
Printed in Singapore by Utopia Press Pte Ltd

Contents

Contributors

Greg Chaikin, formerly Associate Professor at Shimonoseki University, Japan, is currently a Ph.D. candidate in the Department of Political Science and International Studies, University of Queensland, Australia.

Derek Johnson is Senior Researcher at the Center for Maritime Research, Amsterdam, The Netherlands.

Hasjim Djalal is Special Advisor to the Minister, Indonesian Department of Maritime Affairs and Fisheries, Jakarta, Indonesia.

P. Mukundan is Director, ICC International Maritime Bureau, United Kingdom.

Gerard Graham Ong is Research Associate in the Regional Strategic and Political Studies Programme at the Institute of Southeast Asian Studies, Singapore.

Erika Pladdet is a Ph.D. candidate at Erasmus University, Rotterdam, The Netherlands.

Mark J. Valencia is a Maritime Policy Analyst based in Hawaii, USA.

Adam J. Young completed his M.A. in Asian Studies at the University of Hawaii, USA.

INTRODUCTION
Research on Southeast Asian Piracy

Derek Johnson, Erika Pladdet and Mark J. Valencia

Overview

Over the past decade, considerable attention in the media has been devoted to the problem of maritime piracy, particularly as it has been manifested in the waters of Southeast Asia. This renewed attention to piracy reflects reports of a resurgence in armed attacks on vessels at sea by the International Maritime Organization (IMO) and by the International Maritime Bureau (IMB). Surprisingly, while the upsurge in piracy has attracted considerable attention from governments, military experts, and the media, the record of academic publication on piracy in the region is relatively sparse.

The intent of the series of which this volume is the first instalment is to foster new and innovative academic research and writing on the topic of piracy, particularly in Asia. As a foundational volume, this book has the function of bridging the existing efforts piracy studies and the new programme of research and publication that will underpin the series on piracy. The first task of this volume is thus to provide an overview of current knowledge and key themes in Southeast Asian piracy studies in order to provide a reference resource for those working on the topic. The second task is to indicate, in a preliminary manner, important new avenues for research, including those as yet untraveled.

In its role of providing an overview of the field, the volume has brought together contributions that are grounded in the core concerns of piracy studies. As most non-journalistic material on contemporary piracy is from the perspective of international organizations or by academics writing in the context of international relations, this volume is composed of mainly contributions from these two areas. Writing on contemporary piracy returns repeatedly to definitions of piracy, the incidence of piracy, the forms of piracy, and the methods for its suppression. The papers that follow are not exceptions to this pattern. In order to reinforce the centrality of these concerns and to provide a useful reference point, we begin with a review.

Definitions and Concerns in Contemporary Piracy Studies

What is Piracy?

The word pirate derives from the Greek "peirates", which was the label for an adventurer who attacked a ship.[1] Central to any definition of piracy is the association with the sea. This is brought out clearly by the English criminologist Vagg, who states that piracy is equivalent to robbery or banditry with the sole difference that it occurs on water.[2] In practice, piracy is similar to banditry, which is armed robbery using violence or the threat of violence in remote areas outside of effective government control. Thus much contemporary piracy takes place in areas, particularly in developing countries, where authorities are unable or unwilling to intervene.

In contemporary discussions of piracy, the International Maritime Organization and the International Maritime Bureau have a dominant role in defining piracy and setting the counter-piracy agenda as they are the key international organizations involved in anti-piracy activities. The IMO is a specialized organization within the United Nations that has the mandate to develop international standards for promoting safe and environmentally sound shipping activities. The IMB, a part of the International Chamber of Commerce (ICC), established the Anti-Piracy Centre (APC) in Kuala Lumpur, Malaysia, for the explicit purpose of reducing the incidence of piracy. In defining piracy, both organizations emphasize that piracy involves an attack on a ship. This focus on ships runs counter to historical usage that included attacks on settlements by maritime marauders. In the past, pirate activities were directed as much to coastal raiding as to attacks on ships. Raids for booty and slaves triggered the depopulation of entire coastlines.[3] With the political, economic, and military development of coastal areas, such raiding gradually declined to the point where it has practically ceased. While coastal raiding might at some point again become an issue, current political conditions make the IMO-IMB focus on ships reasonable.

Although the IMO and the IMB agree that piracy involves an attack on a ship, their definitions of piracy differ significantly in other ways. The IMO follows the 1982 United Nations Convention on the Law of the Sea (1982 UNCLOS), which in its article 101 declares piracy a criminal act. The 1982 UNCLOS definition of piracy contains five elements. First, piracy must involve a criminal act of violence, detention, or depredation. Second, piracy must be committed on the high seas or in a place outside the jurisdiction of any state. This aspect of the definition flows directly from the idea of *mare liberum*, or open sea, propounded by Hugo de Groot in 1609. De Groot considered the sea to be *res communis*, or the joint property of humankind, serving as the basis of free trade between nations. Piracy endangers the mare liberum and is considered *hostis humani generis*, or an enemy of the common interest of humanity. The concept of mare liberum thus became a key part of maritime common law. This restriction of the definition of piracy to acts on the high seas means that an alternative term has to be created for attacks against ships within territorial waters. The IMO thus defines criminal attacks with weapons on ships within territorial waters as armed robbery and not as piracy. States themselves may or may not have laws that equate acts of armed robbery within their own territorial waters with piracy.[4] The third element of the 1982 UNCLOS definition of piracy is the two-ship requirement. Pirates need to use a ship to attack another ship, which excludes mutiny and privateering from being acts of piracy. Fourth, piracy needs to be committed for private ends, which excludes the acts of terrorists or environmental activists from being piracy. Fifth, attacks by naval craft fall outside the bounds of piracy because pirate attacks have to be committed by the crew or passengers of privately owned vessels.

The IMB defines piracy as "an act of boarding or attempting to board any ship with the intent to commit theft or any other crime and with the attempt or capability to use force in furtherance of that act".[5] This definition makes no distinction between attacks on the high seas and in territorial waters. The two-ship requirement is abolished, which means that attacks from a raft or even from the quay are acts of piracy. The IMB definition does not require that the act of piracy be committed for private ends. Attacks on a ship for political or environmental reasons qualify as piracy. The Achille Lauro incident in 1985 was thus piracy according to the IMB definition.[6] Even the acts of government navy vessels could in certain circumstances conceivably be deemed to be piracy. While choosing either the IMO or IMB definition is not necessary here, we favour the more inclusive IMB definition of piracy. It is true, however, that the distinction between high seas and territorial seas must be considered when conceiving responses to piracy.[7]

The Magnitude of Contemporary Piracy

It is impossible to determine the precise magnitude of contemporary piracy, whether according to the broader IMB definition or the narrower IMO version. Both organizations register pirate attacks according to their own definitions of piracy and publish reports on an annual basis. As attacks have to be reported to the IMB (directly) or to the IMO (indirectly), data on the frequency of piracy attacks depends entirely on the collaboration of crew and captain of the victim vessel, owners/operators, flag states and coastal authorities. Victim vessels can report directly to the IMB, coastal authorities and owners and or operators Flag State. All of them can report indirectly to the IMO (IMO MSC/Circ. 662/p. 7 appendix 1). Each of these groups has specific reasons not to want to register pirate attacks.[8]

For crew and shipping companies, an important reason underpinning the failure to report pirate attacks is the fear of complex reporting procedures. A delay of just one day can cost EUR 10,000 of extra harbour fees and fuel costs.[9] Shipping companies also fear having to pay import duties for the cargo stolen from them.[10] They also often doubt the integrity and competence of local authorities. In such situations they consider it senseless to report their losses because no investigation will be made to track down the pirates or lost cargo.[11] Mistrust is fed by the suspiciously accurate information pirates often have about ship layouts and cargo; information that could quite possibly have come from local authorities who inspect ships and possess detailed information on who and what is present on board.[12] Finally, shipping owners or operators may be reluctant to make such reports due to concern for their commercial reputations. However, one important reason to report pirate attacks to the local authorities is the requirement to do so by insurance companies. Readiness to report pirate incidents thus varies between countries as does the ability and willingness of local, regional, and national authorities to co-operate with the IMB or IMO. Local authorities are sometimes themselves hesitant to contact the IMO or IMB for fear of the economic consequences of their region being declared a high-risk zone.

Victims can report directly to the IMB, owners/operators, flag states and coastal authorities, all of them can report indirectly to the IMO. Owners or operators may still be reluctant to make such reports due to concern for their commercial reputations. Authorities and owners and operators are aware, however, that the benefits of reporting incidents of piracy to the IMO and IMB allows the latter to post warnings about dangerous areas or to distribute information on stolen cargo and vessels (IMO MSC/Circ. 662/p. 7 appendix 1).

Figure I.1 represents an overview of all the incidents of piracy and armed robbery registered by the IMO in the period 1984–2003. It shows an increase in the number of registered piracy attacks between 1994 and 2000,

FIGURE I.1
Incidents of Piracy and Armed Robbery, 1984–2003

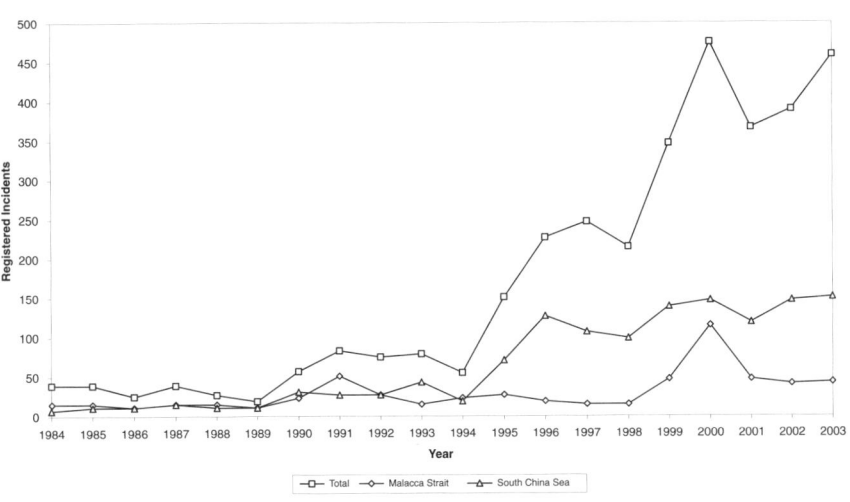

Source: IMO. 2004. Reports on acts of piracy and armed robbery against ships, annual reports 2001 and 2003. London.

a trend which was paralleled in the South China Sea and in the Malacca Strait. These are the most piracy prone areas in the world, with the waters of Indonesia being recognized as the most dangerous in the world.[13] As Mukundan and others in this volume demonstrate, the toll of piracy in terms of injury and death for mariners is serious.

Contemporary Forms of Piracy

Pirate operations vary according to local conditions, the availability of targets, and the competence of the pirates involved. Geography has a large influence on pirate tactics. Attacks on the high seas outside territorial waters are relatively rare because of the greater distances involved and the need for powerful and expensive speedboats. Sea areas dotted with islands, rocks, and reefs form an ideal setting for pirates using the "hit and run" or "Asian" method because they provide hiding places and narrow sea-lanes slow ships down, making them easier targets.[14] Pirates conducting a hit and run attack board a steaming vessel, plunder it, and carry off whatever they have been able to lay their hands on. The geography of Indonesia is particularly propitious for this type of attack. An example of a hit and run attack is that on the oil tanker the Valiant Carrier, as has been vividly described by the journalist Burnett.[15] Attackers boarded the vessel while it was steaming off the coast of Sumatra, foolishly lit a fire on deck, and beat up crewmembers and the captain before disembarking without having managed to steal anything.

The best opportunities for small-scale pirate attacks are offered in and around harbours. Due to congested harbours, ships have to wait a long time, sometimes even days, before entering port. While waiting, they are prey to pirates in small boats. Ships are also vulnerable to being boarded when docked. In both situations, money, cargo, and personal belongings of the persons on board are at risk of theft.[16] Generally, such attacks are by petty criminals and relatively random and disorganized. This type of piracy is particularly common in Africa and South America.[17]

Professional pirates who operate on a long-term basis require much greater organizational sophistication. One important reason for this is their need to procure and operate the modern equipment and fast speedboats employed in attacks on large vessels at sea. Equally critical is their need to secure reliable access to markets and, as much as possible, gain the compliance of local authorities.[18] Bribery is the classic route to achieving these goals. In extreme cases, officials may even collude with pirates by providing information on vessels and cargoes in their areas of jurisdiction.[19] Southeast Asian pirates are the world's most organized, sometimes being linked to criminal organizations, which provide established linkages to market and government.[20] Umbrella criminal organizations may also inform pirates about interesting targets.[21] In some circumstances, as discussed by Ong and by Valencia in this volume, pirates may have connections with warlords and political movements that may have connections with terrorists.[22] For professional pirates, theft of cash, personal belongings, and shipboard electronics are usually of secondary interest. Their primary target is the cargo or even the entire vessel, for which they can earn a much greater return.

When pirates steal an entire vessel, their movement is restricted to those few "ports of refuge" which turn a blind eye to their illegal activities. In such places, the identities of ships are transformed: external appearances are altered, they are given new names, and are newly registered in a flag state before leaving the port. A makeover of this order allows the new "phantom ship" to be used quasi-legally or sold for criminal activities.[23]

Table I.1 presents the number of piracy attacks in international and territorial waters and in harbours (1999–2001). Forty-five per cent of all the attacks registered in 2001 were attacks on ships at anchor. A minority of 21 per cent were classified as traditional attacks, or attacks on the high seas, outside of territorial waters. The number of traditionally defined acts

TABLE I.1
Registered Pirate Attacks by Area, 1999–2001

Year	International Waters		Territorial Waters		Harbours	
2003	102	24%	88	21%	232	55%
2002	49	13%	72	19%	262	68%
2001	79	21%	125	34%	166	45%
2000	136	29%	224	48%	111	23%
1999	38	12%	201	65%	70	23%

Source: IMO. 2002 and 2004. Reports on acts of piracy and armed robbery against ships, annual report 2001 and 2003. London.

of piracy declined significantly with the ratification of 1982 UNCLOS and its provisions enlarging territorial waters from 3 to 12 nautical miles. As a result, the strict definition of piracy in the 1982 UNCLOS Article 101, limiting it to attacks on the high seas, misses the greater number of similar such attacks within territorial waters.

Responses to Piracy

The efficacy of anti-piracy efforts is shaped by the international institutional context. Of key importance in shaping responses to piracy is the legacy of 1982 UNCLOS, which has in effect nationalized the responsibility to react to the larger percentage of piracy cases that occur within territorial waters. The investigation, capture, prosecution, and punishment of pirates who commit crimes within national maritime boundaries thus depend on diverse national systems.[24] Indeed, attacks on vessels committed within the jurisdiction of a coastal state are only considered piracy if the national penal code criminalizes them as such.

Although piracy is criminalized by Article 101 of 1982 UNCLOS, responsibility for the pursuit and punishment of pirates who operate in international waters also falls upon national navies and national courts. The navies of all countries are entitled to seize a ship taken by pirates and arrest them according to 1982 UNCLOS Articles 105 to 107. At present the prosecution of pirates depends on national courts, the rulings of which vary considerably. This may change should the new International Criminal Court begin to try piracy cases, as it arguably could do.[25]

There are several instances of regional co-operation for the suppression of piracy. At a regional level, countries are working together to combat piracy. In the Caribbean, Dutch, French, American, British, Jamaican, and Venezuelan naval units and coastguard vessels are working together to confront drug trafficking and piracy.[26] A similar regional effort to combat piracy is proposed for the South China Sea but due to limited budgets, overlapping jurisdictions, sovereignty concerns, and a lack of effective extradition procedures, its implementation is lagging.[27] Finally, occasional joint patrols of the Japanese coastguard with those of India and Malaysia were instituted following an anti-piracy conference in Tokyo in 2000.[28]

National and regional efforts to control piracy are of course supported by significant international informational resources from the IMO and

IMB. Both provide invaluable data gathering services and co-ordination activities. Among its most important contributions to maritime security, the IMO has helped improve inter-ship communication systems and has developed piracy response protocols for crew. Currently it is developing the International Ship and Port Facility Security Code (ISPS Code), which contains detailed security related requirements for governments, port authorities, and shipping companies.

Contributions

The reference value of this volume is brought out particularly by papers of Young and Mukundan. Young's paper provides the historical background to piracy in Southeast Asia, a context that he argues is insufficiently considered in understanding the prevalence and characteristics of piracy in the region. He argues that more attention to the context in which piracy occurs, and has developed, would help reorient responses to the underlying causes of piracy such as economic and political marginalization. As professionals with long experience working in the area of ocean security, Mukundan and Djalal's papers provide useful ground-level perspectives. Mukundan, as Director of the International Maritime Bureau, is privy to the most up-to-date statistical and policy matters concerning piracy. His contribution to this volume thus provides a unique official perspective on piracy in Southeast Asian waters. Djalal, a career civil servant in the Indonesian government with considerable diplomatic experience brings his insider's view to bear on piracy in the region.

Beyond providing a solid foundation for the analysis of maritime piracy in Southeast Asia and elsewhere, the second programmatic task of the volume is to identify key themes and research questions that will stimulate a concentrated attempt to consolidate and expand the scope of academic work in this area. The first of such topics examined in depth in this volume is the conflict between the widely acknowledged need for regional collaboration in counter-piracy activities in Southeast Asia and the great realpolitik political barriers to such co-operation. While this is a theme touched on to some degree by all authors, it is the primary focus of the contributions in the fifth and sixth sections of the book by Valencia, Chaikin, and Djalal. Valencia reviews the range of political initiatives to control piracy in the region. He highlights the political challenges of expanding regional co-operation and argues that the most viable approach may be to continue to support ad hoc responses supported by extensive contacts between states at the informal, or Track Two level. Chaikin argues that after years of neglect of the oceans within international relations, awareness has grown in recent decades of the need to engage in the building of co-operative international regimes for addressing such problems as piracy. A foundation has been laid through ASEAN and other institutions in this regard but considerable work remains to be done. Chaikin focuses on the importance of Japan in the maritime security equation in Southeast Asia and suggests that Japan is well positioned to take a leadership role, provided it continues to base its strategy on the use of its civilian coast guard rather than the military. Djalal's contribution is a detailed report on the current status of negotiations for the suppression of piracy in Southeast Asia, with particular emphasis on the concerns of Indonesia, from the perspective of a policy maker with deep knowledge of the intricacies of inter-state relations in the region. He concludes with a series of recommendations for the strengthening of state capacities for the suppression of piracy that could be implemented with enhanced international support and co-operation. Indonesia in particular would benefit from international assistance which builds the country's law enforcement capacity while respecting its territorial sovereignty.

Greatly heightened concern with security in recent years has strongly influenced writing on piracy and has provided the impetus for the second theme to be examined in depth in this volume: the utility of linking piracy with terrorism. Ong argues forcefully that considerable advantage will be gained in the efforts to combat piracy in Southeast Asia if an explicit conceptual link can be made between piracy and terrorism in the minds of policymakers in the region. Doing so could provide the necessary impetus to break the current impasse around several key issues pertinent to piracy suppression. Valencia's article on piracy and maritime terrorism takes a contrary tack to that of Ong by arguing for the importance of distinguishing between piracy and terrorism in Southeast Asia. Each is distinct in terms of *modus operandi* and the groups involved. He argues that conflating the two phenomena could reduce the effectiveness of existing counter-piracy strategies. In the conclusion, other potential topics for research are raised, including some which depart significantly from the currently dominant tendencies in piracy studies.

Notes

1   Brian Innes, *The Book of Pirates: Buccaneers, Corsairs, Privateers, Freebooters, & All Sea Rovers* (London: Bancroft, 1966) and Young, this volume.

2   J. Vagg, "Rough Seas? Contemporary Piracy in South East Asia", *British journal of criminology* 35, no. 1 (1995).

3   J.F. Warren, "A Tale of Two Centuries: The Globalization of Maritime Raiding and Piracy in Southeast Asia at the End of the Eighteenth and Twentieth Centuries", in *KITLV Jubilee Workshop* (Leiden: 2001).

4   Keyuan Zou, "Enforcing the Law of Piracy in the South China Sea", *Journal of Maritime Law and Commerce* 31, no. 1 (2000).

5   J. Abhyankar, *An Overview on Piracy Problems — a Global Update* [HTTP] (1999 [cited 12 February 2003]); available from <http://www.sils.org/seminar/1999-piracy-00.htm>.

6   Ibid. ([cited) and Valencia, "Piracy and Terrorism", this volume.

7   Keyuan Zou, *Issues of Public International Law Relating to the Crackdown of Piracy in the South China Sea and Prospects for Regional Co-operation* (1999 [cited 5 February 2003]); available from <http://www.sils.org/seminar/1999-piracy-00.htm>.

8   Peter Chalk, "Contemporary Marine Piracy in Southeast Asia", *Studies in Conflict and Terrorism* 21 (1998), IMO, "Reports on Acts of Piracy and Armed Robbery against Ships, Annual Report 2001" (London: 2002) but see also Mukundan, this volume.

9   M. Veldt, "Misdaad Op Zee", *Intermediair*, 26 March 1993.

10 H. Jippes, "Moderne Zeepiraten; Yohoho En Een Fles Met Rum", *NRC Handelsblad*, 15 November 1997.

11 W. van der Post, "Geweld Op Zee Neemt Toe; Nederlandse Schepen Vaker Prooi Van Zeerovers", *Algemeen Dagblad*, 5 February 1997.

12 Jippes, "Moderne Zeepiraten; Yohoho En Een Fles Met Rum".

13 International Chamber of Commerce, *Piracy Soars as Violence against Seafarers Intensifies* [Web page] (2003 [cited 30 July 2003]); available from <http://www.iccwbo.org/ccs/news_archives/2003/piracy_report_second_quarter.asp>, see also Mukundan, this volume.

14 Abhyankar, *An Overview on Piracy Problems — a Global Update* (cited).

15 J. Burnett, *Dangerous Waters, Modern Piracy and Terror on the High Seas* (New York: Penguin Group, 2002).

16 Post, "Geweld Op Zee Neemt Toe; Nederlandse Schepen Vaker Prooi Van Zeerovers".

17 Abhyankar, *An Overview on Piracy Problems — a Global Update* (cited).

18 Vagg, "Rough Seas? Contemporary Piracy in South East Asia", J.L. Worral, "The Routine Activities of Maritime Piracy", *Security Journal* (2000).

[19]   Worral, "The Routine Activities of Maritime Piracy".
[20]   C. Stellweg, "Zeepiraten Terug Van Weggeweest", *Algemeen Dagbad* (1999).
[21]   M. Christern, "Zeerovers Vonden Vrijhaven in China", *NRC Handelsblad*, 15 February 1999.
[22]   Burnett, *Dangerous Waters, Modern Piracy and Terror on the High Seas.*
[23]   Chalk, "Contemporary Marine Piracy in Southeast Asia", Jippes, "Moderne Zeepiraten; Yohoho En Een Fles Met Rum."
[24]   Zou, "Enforcing the Law of Piracy in the South China Sea".
[25]   Zou, *Issues of Public International Law Relating to the Crackdown of Piracy in the South China Sea and Prospects for Regional Co-operation* (cited).
[26]   F.N.J. Jansen, "De Caribische Zee, Een Zee Vol Juridische Onzekerheden", 31, no. 1 (2000).
[27]   Zou, "Enforcing the Law of Piracy in the South China Sea".
[28]   See Chaikin, this volume.

1

Roots of Contemporary Maritime Piracy in Southeast Asia[1]

Adam J. Young

Introduction

Much research has been directed at examining contemporary maritime piracy in Southeast Asia from the perspectives of maritime security, as a non-traditional security threat, a "grey area phenomenon", and through non-traditional security theory such as "human security".[2] This research has provided many useful insights into the nature of contemporary piracy in Southeast Asia, and is at the heart of a growing effort to combat this resurgent phenomenon. However historical context is often lacking, or treated in broad generalizations, surreptitiously linking phenomena over vast stretches of time.[3] Moreover, there appears to be little attempt in modern piracy literature dealing with Southeast Asia to conceptualize piracy within the socio-political and cultural framework of Southeast Asia itself. In particular, authors frequently try to reconcile Southeast Asian piracy, currently the most prolific in the world, through definitions of piracy that evolved in a particular Western colonial and legal tradition.[4] Similarly, historical accounts of piracy are frequently isolated from contemporary circumstances, making them quite literally "academic" in their application to policy.[5]

In order to better understand contemporary manifestations of piracy in Southeast Asia, and the context from which it has emerged, the historical context of piracy and its links to modern piracy need to be more fully explored. Some notable works in recent years have moved in this direction.[6] However, the majority of both academic and policy literature on piracy seems largely uninformed about the other. This chapter seeks to help bridge the gap between historical context and policy analysis, and from this broader understanding, suggest ways and means of addressing the root causes of contemporary maritime piracy in Southeast Asia.

Contemporary maritime piracy in Southeast Asia has been heavily influenced by modern economic, political, and social forces. Processes of globalization, with its high speed information networks linking parties across the globe, expanding economic development, and growing interdependence, are shaping the modern world, including piracy. However, contemporary piracy did not evolve in a vacuum separated from historical context. Indeed maritime piracy has been a reality in Southeast Asia since at least the fifth century C.E, when a Chinese pilgrim returning home from India via Southeast Asia mentioned piracy in the Strait of Malacca.[7] The activities being referred to as piracy 1,500 years ago were an intrinsic part of a complex social web, with elements of political and economic competition, as well as social status, common through much of maritime Southeast Asia.[8] Piracy has waxed and waned over the centuries according to the flow of local and global trade, and the power of regional polities to control this trade and exert their influence in the region. This is particularly exemplified by the the competition over expanding trade, from the fifth century as the Srivijayan Kingdom emerged in the southern reaches of the Strait of Malacca, to the nineteenth century, and more recently, over the last 30 years as Southeast Asia has experienced rapid economic development. In all these eras piracy has existed beyond the control of any state. But why has piracy persisted in Southeast Asia from the remote fifth century to today? What are the continuities linking past and present? What are the discontinuities that establish each form of "piracy" as a unique manifestation of its times? What allowed piracy to thrive in the past, and why has it resurfaced as a significant security concern today? What are the roots of contemporary maritime piracy in Southeast Asia, and what do the answers to these questions suggest in the way of responses to its contemporary manifestation? These are some of the questions this chapter will try to address.

Western and Southeast Asian Cultural and Historical Contexts of Piracy

The Western Context

Defining "piracy" is problematic. Indeed the word piracy has been variously used to describe everything from enemy combatants to common criminals.[9] The complexity of the term piracy as a social construct would appear to make analysis of actual phenomena labelled as piracy problematic. But analysing how understandings differ, and how they have changed over time and place, provides a way to avoid some of the biases in the use of the term.[10] To many of us piracy seems straightforward. The word conjures up images of swashbuckling adventurers from Hollywood blockbusters, dastardly villains in the form of Black Beard (Edward Thatch), Long John Silver and the like. To ordinary people they are robbers operating at sea, to be hunted down, tried in a court of law and punished.

However, as with any concept that is the arbitrary product of subjective values, the definition of piracy is malleable and fluid, adapted to different cultures, politics and times. Piracy should be thought of not as a "thing", static in its moral judgment, but as a concept given to change over time, and through experience as Campo has termed it as "a concept in development."[11]

The term piracy in the Western tradition derives from ancient Roman and Greek concepts which did not originally include a sense of criminality, unlike modern interpretations of the word. The word *"peirato"* connoting political legitimacy and belligerency, applied to peoples of the eastern Mediterranean, i.e., those *included* under the growing Roman hegemony. While those deemed *"pirata"*[12] were people who pursued a way of life *outside* of that Roman hegemony and were therefore illegitimate.

Particularly important are certain concepts in the law of piracy, such as criminality,[13] *"animo furandi"*,[14] and *"hostes humani generis"*,[15] which evolved from subsequent interpretations of ancient classical literature. During Medieval times and the early Renaissance, the word *pirata* changed in meaning from belligerent, in the context of war, to un-authorized privateer. This term was used pejoratively to describe one who seized ships and goods, but such risks were accepted as a cost of participating in the burgeoning trade of the times, and it was not yet legally criminalized.

Renaissance publicists and jurists such as the Dutch Hugo Grotius (1583–1645), who is often termed the father of modern international law, the Italian Alberico Gentilis (1552–1608), and the British John Selden (1584–1654), drew heavily on these classic texts to support their postulations of international law. These sixteenth and seventeenth century legal minds, however, introduced a novel legal interpretation of the word *pirata* to describe specific cases of maritime violence outside the bounds of law, i.e. criminal acts. Gentilis specifically describes how piracy, (using the Latin *pirata*) without the consent of the king, is equivalent to brigandage or banditry on land.[16] Similarly, Grotius postulated that piracy in "natural" law, i.e., laws common to all nature and those in it, that the "...word [piracy] would fit robber bands on sea or on land."[17]

Thus the use of the Latin word *pirata* through the sixteenth and seventeenth centuries, including its translation into English municipal law, was increasingly at odds with the classical texts. This subtle shift in meaning had important ramifications, as "pirates" became not belligerents in war, but common robbers. Yet the concept of *hostes humanis generis* seems to have persisted.[18] Additionally, the concept of *animo furandi*, which had been applied to the words *"latrones"* and *"praedones"* (bandits and robbers), was applied to the new understanding of piracy. Thus piracy suggested a theft for private gain, like a robber, but was now a crime against all humankind because it was on the seas and not directed against any one target group. This confusion of *praedones* and *pirata*, or robber and pirate, and their associated legal contexts had a great impact on future development of international law dealing with piracy.[19]

Grotius, Gentilis, and Selden were reinterpreting concepts of international law at a time when the economic and political dynamics of European states were changing rapidly. Grotius, employed by the Dutch government, was in part seeking to justify expanding Dutch commercial interests in the East Indies, and thus justified protecting this commerce by the harshest means. Grotius conceived of piracy as a criminal disturbance of lawful commerce and a state's sovereignty. Thus jurisdiction could be extended through naval occupation of waters, just as in the military occupation of land, which provided the impetus for justifying martial action to protect commerce.[20] Gentillis interpreted piracy as being linked to the license of a respective monarch, so that unrecognized maritime raiding was seen as criminal, not an act of war. Under *hostes humani generis*, "pirates" were the enemy of all humankind and not legally entitled to belligerent status. This interpretation gave any given monarch the right to extend their municipal criminal law to the seas, and to punish anyone obstructing their commerce who did not have a licence from a ruler that was recognized by the said state.[21] Likewise, Selden's classic *Mare Clausum* was aimed at extending a particular interpretation of maritime law, which would allow England to claim parts of the seas in a quasi-occupation,[22] and thus extend their municipal jurisdiction in the seas. Selden, and subsequent British legalists had great influence on the laws of piracy, particularly because England became the dominant European power of the sea in the mid-nineteenth century following the defeat of the French navy outside the Spanish port of Cadiz, off Cape Trafalgar at the hands of Vice-Admiral Horatio Lord Nelson. This dominance lasted until the end of the age of sail.[23]

Complicating European practice and understandings of piracy as a criminal activity, was the wide use of privateers. Privateers in international law were defined as "vessels belonging to private owners, and sailing under commission of war empowering the person to whom it is granted to carry on all forms of hostility which are permissible at sea by the usages of war."[24] This included seizure of goods and property, and contrasted with the definition of piracy as an act carried out by "...a body of men acting independently of any politically organized society."[25] The use of privateers to supplement the meagre naval forces of cash strapped states in time of war was a standard practice among Western states, from the thirteenth century to the nineteenth century. Privateers were a resource of highly skilled mariners that the state did not have to pay for, and could actually provide revenue for the state, as a portion of their prizes was generally given to the state.[26]

Empowering non-state actors with legitimatized means of violence, however, had its dangers, as it often proved difficult to rein in privateers once their purpose had been served. As a result of the frequent wars in Europe at the time, combined with the practice of privateering, piracy in European waters, extending from the Mediterranean to the English Channel, became rampant by the seventeenth century.[27] During times of war, "pirates" and other such sea folk were granted pardons and given commissions to fight his or her majesties' war, but when the war ended, these "pirates", now pardoned, were turned loose with no means of making a living. Many turned back to piracy until the next war, and the cycle would begin again. As Daniel Defoe noted as early as the beginning of the eighteenth century: "Privateers in time of war are a nursery for Pyrates against a Peace."[28] Ironically privateering "…evolved into a weapon of the weak…as in the case of the United States and Britain during the war of 1812," despite being "…invented and encouraged by the "strong" states of Europe [Britain, France, Spain]."[29] Not only the United States, but Southeast Asian raiding practices may also be seen as privateering; an effective weapon of the "weak" when facing the British Navy. For this reason, in the nineteenth century, when Britain had become *the* naval power in the world, privateering was finally outlawed by the majority of European naval powers at Britain's behest, through the Declaration of Paris in 1858 following the end of the Crimean War.[30] The law of "piracy" continued to evolve in the municipal law codes of European countries and the United States, but the basic principals did not change significantly.

This evolution of the concept of piracy led directly to the definition of piracy incorporated in the 1958 Geneva Conventions on Law of the Sea and the 1982 United Nations Convention of the Law of the Sea (UNCLOS).

Article 101 of UNCLOS defines piracy as follows:

Article 101
Definition of piracy
piracy consists of any of the following acts:
(a) any illegal acts of violence or detention, or any act of depredation, committed for private ends by the crew or the passengers of a private ship or a private aircraft, and directed:
  (i) on the high seas, against another ship or aircraft, or against persons or property on board such ship or aircraft;
  (ii) against a ship, aircraft, persons or property in a place outside the jurisdiction of any State;
(b) any act of voluntary participation in the operation of a ship or of an aircraft with knowledge of facts making it a pirate ship or aircraft;
(c) any act of inciting or of intentionally facilitating an act described in subparagraph (a) or (b).[31]

And the definition is still evolving. For example, the International Maritime Bureau defines piracy as: "An act of boarding or attempting to board any ship with the intent to commit theft or any other crime and with the intent or capability to use force in the furtherance of that act."[32] This definition sidesteps the issues of private gain, high seas, and the involvement of two ships, that were troublesome aspects of the 1982 UNCLOS definition, and has thus even broadened the scope of "piracy."

The Southeast Asian Context

Piracy/raiding has existed in maritime Southeast Asia at least since there were people to record it, and likely existed prior to that despite there being no literate society there to document it. But, defining piracy becomes even more problematic when considered in the context of Southeast Asia, as there are many layers of labels and translations that have accumulated over the centuries. Unfortunately, historical forms of piracy were predominantly documented by foreigners passing through Southeast Asia. Each group had their own religious, economic, and political agendas, and their own unique way of making sense of what they saw and translating it into their own languages. Thus understanding and describing Southeast Asian predatory maritime activities from the perspective of outsiders presents inherent difficulties. Even though Europeans left more copious documentation of piracy, and their colonial history in Southeast Asia has made their influence that much stronger, they were not the first to apply labels to this phenomenon.

In the early fifth century[33] Shih Fa-Hsien (the "Buddhist" "Illustrious in Law") travelled through Southeast Asia on his way home to China from a pilgrimage to the holy centres of Buddhism in India. Fa-Hsien wrote about the passage through the Strait of Malacca: "This sea is infested with pirates, to meet whom is death."[34] It is unclear if he himself witnessed any incidents or simply heard second hand, but the characters from the text used by Wheatley could mean robber, or thief, but could also mean rebel.[35] However, from the previous characters, the context is set in the ocean, so it was translated as the English word "pirate". Another record, this one from the later eighth and early ninth centuries, a geographical memoir compiled by Chia-Tan, notes amongst various descriptions of Southeast Asian kingdoms a place where "The inhabitants are mostly pirates."[36] This passage, coming two hundred years later, uses different characters than the previous passage (not unusual since Chinese was phonetic and not standardized until this century), and has a meaning comprised of two characters that literally mean "those who do violence",[37] and again has been translated as the English "pirate". Accounts of Arab travellers and historians, some of whom like Ibn Battutah might have actually travelled to Southeast Asia, and not just collected stories from Persian ports, also mention piracy. Ibn Battutah, writing in the mid fourteenth century, in one passage mentions junks getting ready for "...piratical raids, and also to deal with any junks that might attempt to resist their exactions, for they exact tribute on each junk [calling at that place]."[38] This account would seem to describe Southeast Asian piracy more in terms of extraction of taxes rather than as simple sea robbery.

Another layer of meaning is added by local words for maritime predatory activities, such as the Malay *rompak* (the action) and *perompak* (the person doing the action) connoting traditional maritime predatory activities, which according to the 1959 Wilkinson Malay/English Dictionary translates as "Piracy; robbery on the waters (v II, 980)." Trocki further elucidates the term *perompak* as "wanderers and renegades who included hereditary outlaw bands with no fixed abode,"[39] and notes the political and commercial significance of the practice.[40] This suggests a clear concept of legitimate and illegitimate raiding practices, one under the control of a ruler, the other not. Later in the seventeenth and eighteenth centuries, as the raids of the Iranun stemming from the Sulu Sultanate in what is now the southern Philippines became widespread, their name itself was often alliterated to "*lanun*" or "*Ilanun*", becoming a word describing a particular style of piracy characterized by large raiding vessels, armed with dozens of men and cannon (Wilkinson 1959, p. 655). This style of raiding, in comparison to that of local sea people, is vividly recounted in the *Tuhfat al-Nafis*, which describes an assault on an Illanun stronghold in Riau, noting their larger boats, armed with numerous cannons, and their more intensive raiding patterns.[41] These local words suggest an antiquity and durability of predatory activities, as well as active processes of change, as new terms are added to include new forms of raiding/piracy.

These words have come down through the ages, and have been picked from a plethora of indigenous terms, to be included in our dictionaries where they have negative connotations in their English translations, but are not representative of all understandings of predatory maritime activities. Many traditional heroes, respected for their courage and moral examples, were "pirates". For example, in the Philippines "...raiders were regarded as popular heroes and enjoyed inter-island reputations...Their exploits became the stuff of local legend, and the most famous among them were...worthy of being memorialized in...heroic epics...."[42] Likewise in

the Malay world, raiding could be an honorable occupation, being "...widely regarded as a suitable occupation for a prince whose income was insufficient to meet his needs."[43] One example is Raja Ismail, a notable *anak raja* (child of a king or ruler) and mystical hero, in the mid-eighteenth century, who was one of various factions competing for control of the Siak Sultanate, after its separation from Johor early in the sixteenth century. This *anak raja* gained a royal following and sought his fortunes at sea, largely through raiding a "...common practice throughout the region, but Siak princes raised it to new heights, using it to create their own *negeri* [state, or polity] and bases of authority."[44] Even European accounts acknowledged the "heroic" aspect of Southeast Asian pirates. For example, a seventeenth century Dutch account of the life of La Ma'dukelleng Arung Sikang, described him as a "prince of pirates" (*raja bajak laut*) who became the ruler of the Buginese state of Wajo in southern Sulawesi in the late sixteenth and seventeenth centuries.[45]

In the Philippines, complex societies existed at the time of first European contact, where raiding was "The most celebrated form of ...warfare...," called *mangayaw*, a word found in all the major languages of the Philippines.[46] The intricacies of raiding, its important roles in those societies, and the widespread nature of similar traditions suggest that it was a practice of great diversity and depth in the region.

Traditionally piracy/raiding in Southeast Asia served a variety of socially constructive purposes. Unlike European piracy, Southeast Asian piracy/raiding did not generally involve "criminal" elements. Nor was it typically a rebellion against society and its laws. Therefore it was not outside civilization as *hostes humani generis*, but instead incorporated into the laws of society. This does not mean that all raiding was legitimate, as both the *Tufat al-Nafis* and the account of La Ma'dukelleng both suggest. Ahmad frequently describes punishments meted out to raiders operating without consent from the ruler,[47] and La Ma'dukelleng was reported to have committed a host of transgressions before he became the ruler of Wajo.[48] These practices did have legitimate forms, however, that were important to the societies that practised them.

As Tarling notes, "Robbery and violence indeed existed, but to describe them as piracy attributed them to lesser motives than in the light of history, may often be fairly suggested for them."[49] It was normally the most respected warriors and leaders of traditional societies engaged in a competitive prestige system that participated in maritime raiding, not the wretched poor or hardened criminals typically associated with Atlantic and Caribbean piracy.[50] Raiding/piracy was a part of the social fabric and accordingly interacted with politics, economics, and spirituality. Motivations were not necessarily only for material gain, even if raids often brought material wealth. The ubiquity and cultural significance of raiding might make it appear to be an unchanging tradition in maritime Southeast Asia, part of a primordial constant over the centuries. However, raiding/piracy were dynamic traditions that underwent change as societies and cultures in the region changed. For instance, from the mid-eighteenth century through the nineteenth century, the European presence in the region altered trading patterns and provoked dramatic changes in the socio-political make up of the region, fragmenting political control.[51] In the Malay world, raiding also became fragmented since it was no longer under the control of major political centres, the profits of raiding began to accrue to specific leaders.

Local understandings of Southeast Asian maritime predatory activities were eventually changed by the coming of Europeans, beginning in the sixteenth century. Through the processes of imperialism and colonialism, particularly in the later half of the eighteenth and nineteenth centuries, European concepts of piracy of the time were overlaid on local traditions, criminalizing traditional maritime predatory activities. Thus the layers of meaning and interpretation applied to predatory maritime activities in Southeast Asia have blurred their original meanings, confusing the contexts from which they came. Even today, contemporary definitions of piracy are problematic when applied to Southeast Asia.[52] It is thus with caution that the word piracy, with all its implications and contemporary understandings, should be applied to phenomena in widely different times, places, and cultures.[53] Indeed, in the words of Nicholas Tarling, referring to Van Leur's cautionary words about applying European standards and categories to Southeast Asia: "In a sense this warning applies also to the concept of piracy which carries from its European context certain standards of meaning and overtones which render inexact its application even to ostensibly comparable Asian phenomenon."[54] This English word, derived from thousands of years of evolutionary usage, has been used to describe varying dynamic traditional practices spanning approximately 1500 years in Southeast Asia.

The concept of piracy is thus complex and defining the term both from a Western perspective, and in Southeast Asian contexts, is rather problematic. Historic manifestations of piracy in Southeast Asia were quite heterogeneous, encompassing a broad range of socio-political-cultural motives, and an equally diverse range of actual practice. Foreign accounts of some of these activities, although it is questionable if any of the early authors directly witnessed an actual attack, describe them as piracy or at least that is the English translation of the Chinese and Arabic sources. European accounts and understandings of local predatory maritime activities in the sixteenth and following centuries, had the greatest impact on how the outside world saw these activities, and eventually redefined how local power structures also viewed them. Through the processes of expanding imperialist activities, and eventually colonialism by the nineteenth century, European power in maritime Southeast Asia allowed the imposition of Western legal perspectives on local political and social phenomenon. In this context, the diverse local practices and traditions, both "legitimate" and "illegitimate" in the eyes of local power structures, were included in the Western term and conception of piracy, and made a criminal offence unacceptable to any Western defined civil society.

Thus the Western concept of piracy eclipsed any other official concept of the word, and became the foundation of international law. Nevertheless, these definitions and understandings, as in the past, do not entirely fit the reality of piracy. They do not take into account the local context of piracy in maritime Southeast Asia, and thus create a conceptual gap in our understanding of the phenomena, and interfere with attempts to address piracy in the region. Contexualizing piracy specifically within maritime Southeast Asia will provide a better understanding of the phenomenon, including both its historic roots and its contemporary manifestations. This will in turn facilitate the process of comparative analysis between past and present phenomena, from which insight for addressing contemporary maritime piracy in Southeast Asia may be derived.

Approaches to the Issues

The study of piracy is fraught with epistemological problems, as with "...the word "crime" itself ...piracy is a term that both describes and passes a (negative) judgment...addresses an object that is *a priori* normatively defined, and is based primarily on sources in which this value judgment goes without saying."[55] Although the literature used for this chapter by and large is grounded in a negative *a priori* assessment of piracy, there have been several notable attempts to portray piracy without moralizing, and yet trying not to minimize the brutal reality of piracy in its various forms across the centuries.[56] This objective stance is all the more important because the topic of maritime piracy in Southeast Asia is viewed in a context largely outside of the academic roots of Western scholarship. It is thus important to consider that while trying to unravel the layers of interpretation of Southeast Asian piracy, this chapter uses a vocabulary that is rooted in a particular academic, cultural paradigm.

Post-modern critiques, and the whole debate surrounding Orientalism that the late Edward Said championed, make us more aware of using outside definitions to describe foreign phenomenon such as piracy in Southeast Asia. As Said suggests, however, while it is impossible to divorce oneself from one's intellectual heritage totally, the effort can be made to free one's research from biases,[57] and in the case of piracy a self-conscious awareness of indigenous perspectives can help alleviate this situation. This goal is somewhat complicated, however, by the ubiquitous complaint and fact that indigenous sources are scarce in Southeast Asia. Accounts of Southeast Asian piracy largely derive from foreign sources: Chinese, Arabic, and later, European. In this situation judicious use of foreign accounts and ethnographic studies is quite helpful, but still problematic for trying to understand piracy in Southeast Asia.

Historically each social group in maritime Southeast Asia, engaging in raiding/piracy, had their own unique practices which performed a variety of functions. Similarly, contemporary piracy manifests itself in numerous forms: from low end "hit and run" thefts, where "pirates" sneak aboard ships and grab what they can lay their hands on with an average cash value of $5,000 to $15,000; to short term seizures of vessels often involving weapons and at least short term hostage taking; and even to hijacking of entire vessels, the selling of their cargos, the disposing of their crew, and the use of the ship to commit further crimes.[58] Yet through this diversity there are tempting and undeniable undercurrents of similarity across the diverse geography of people and place, as well as across time.

An intriguing aspect of indigenous and European concepts of piracy, both historically and contemporarily, is the role of the state in encouraging and controlling piracy. State control reflects the dynamic tension between acts of piracy and their asserted political legitimacy or legality, which is at the heart of a subjective term like piracy. Contemporary piracy would seem to exist as a clearly illegitimate maritime activity in the agreed upon system of modern states, laws, and international relations, based on Weberian principals of power, authority, and legitimacy, which gives states monopolistic control of the means of coercive force.[59] But those agents intimately involved in piracy may perceive their actions differently. Historically this was certainly the case, as the boundaries between "state" and "non-state" were frequently blurred, and state structures often actively encouraged and supported non-state agents of violence, like privateers or raiders, when their activities were to the benefit of the political centre.[60] However, this tenuous control was often disregarded by non-state agents and they often acted relatively independently of state power, until they could be brought back under control again.[61] State control is a dynamic of power, dependent on who has the authority, to determine political legitimacy and illegitimacy[62] through force, or agreement and assent of the nation. The present nation state system in Southeast Asia formed through hundreds of years of interaction, competition, and negotiation between various local polities and European powers. The process of this evolution has left its imprint on the present structure, including the conceptual and structural elements of piracy.

Beyond establishing the *post facto* legitimacy or illegitimacy of piracy, state control is also a fundamental consideration in the physical enactment of piracy, i.e., the states ability to exert some minimal control of the people in its territory through "…binding commands, rules, and laws backed by force," and reciprocal social contracts, thereby controlling those who become the agents of piracy.[63] This includes the state's ability to maintain political authority, and therein maintain its claim to a monopoly of the means of legitimate coercive violence, and the ability to regulate illegitimate violence, as well as controlling and regulating available technology and restricting access to those technologies that pose a threat to the state.

The increase in indigenous piracy (much of which was organized raiding), during the latter half of the eighteenth century through the first half of the nineteenth century, resulted in part from changes in the economic and political structures of maritime Southeast Asia that had started with the Portuguese conquest of Malacca in 1511,[64] but which were also simply an extension of indigenous political, social, and cultural processes. Raiding and piracy went virtually unchecked for almost a century, from the late eighteenth well into the nineteenth century, as European powers struggled to overcome difficulties at home, such as the Napoleonic Wars that ravaged Europe from 1799–1815, and to find local alliances and partners that were willing to co-operate in achieving their economic and political goals in the region.

By the mid-nineteenth century, several factors started coming together for the European powers, which began to turn the tide against raiders and "pirates." The political turmoil in Europe from earlier in the century had abated allowing more attention to be focused on foreign interests, and thus the colonial powers expanded their presence and formed local alliances, creating a group of local polities in alignment with the ambitions of European powers, and thus willing allies in "suppressing piracy".[65] The rapid economic development of the time was making local and European interests ever convergent.[66] As European political influence in the region expanded, European powers implemented a legal system that now defined legitimate maritime activities, in contrast to the rather more flexible and fluid socio-cultural-political system governing such relations and activities in local polities. Piracy as a criminal act against colonial shipping allowed for action as "policemen" rather than as an act of war, and thus there was a shift from "war between states" to protect commercial interests to "military action to suppress piracy".[67] The idea of piracy as *hostes humani generis*, was extended from British Admiralty and common law, and thus raiding as a form of competition against British commerce was a criminal act, an act of piracy. Similarly, the Spanish in the mid to late nineteenth century used acts of piracy by the Sulu Sultanate to justify their attacks on raiding bases in the region, an opportunity to curtail raids that had devastated much of the central Philippines. In this way piracy provided an excuse, or justification, for foreign powers to extend their influence into Southeast Asian territory. Technological innovations coming out of the industrial revolution in Europe were also of great significance. Innovations in steam power, firearms, and communications allowed European imperialism to expand, creating colonial states, and widening and deepening their control of much of the region.

Despite the persistence of indigenous practices that continued through most of the nineteenth century,[68] by the end of the century they had largely ceased, and maritime competition in the form of raiding was *de facto* eliminated, replaced by "crime" and "rebellion", acts at variance with established colonial state practices. Interaction and negotiation of maritime practice no longer focused on broad competition between rival systems, but now became a matter of what was beyond the reach and control of colonial states. European influence dramatically changed definitions of legitimacy and forever altered power structures in the region. Local states and time honoured raiding practices would no longer be the basis of legitimacy for predatory maritime activities, as colonial powers, and their successors, the independent nation states of Southeast Asia, became the locus of power and authority in the region. Yet piracy persisted throughout the colonial era, evolving and adapting, "It just moved into the interstitial seams between the "sinews" of state power, seeking out places and moments where such attacks had a chance of success."[69]

Lessons from the Past: Continuities and Discontinuities between Historic and Contemporary Piracy

This discussion of discontinuities will emphasize important, broad conceptual differences between historical "piracy" and present day "piracy", ignoring the obvious myriad of details that have changed from the nineteenth century and before. The discussion of continuities will focus on three aspects of state control that are important in understanding both historical and contemporary manifestations of "piracy": state control of people, the agents of "piracy", the state's ability to maintain a political hegemony, and the state's ability to regulate and/or dominate technologies.

Contemporary maritime piracy in Southeast Asia is conceptually very different from its historical roots. The key differences seem to lay in conceptual changes that have stemmed from material, political, social, and cultural change over the last several hundred years, but were most pronounced in the last 150 to 200 years. Local predatory maritime activities evolved as a positive response to this changing environment, but maintained a "traditional" sense of the socio-political-cultural significance of the activity, and thrived well into the nineteenth century. The proliferation of piracy suggested general political instability and "decay" within many states. However, the idea of decay should not be taken too far, for piracy if left to itself, had an ability to reconstitute legitimate political structures, especially during a reshuffling of the power structure. However the instability in economic and political structures in the seventeenth, eighteenth, and nineteenth centuries, largely resulting from European involvement, led to dramatic, lasting changes to fundamental principals of political, economic, and social organization. In this situation the

TABLE 1.1
Piracy Past and Present: Discontinuities and Continuities

Discontinuities

---

1   A distinct definitional and conceptual separation between conditional legitimacy in the past, and complete illegitimacy in the present, has radically changed the nature of piracy.

2   There has been real material, political, social, and cultural change between the nineteenth century and today, which makes the phenomenon called "piracy" in some ways very different.

3   Rigidly defined, static territorial borders have been established through the imposition of Western, Westphalian geopolitical consciousness in maritime Southeast Asia.

Continuities

---

1   "Piracy" is a complex, diverse phenomena, lacking contextualization within Southeast Asia, making definition difficult, and therefore problematizing the addressing of the issue.

2   Despite changes, there is a continuous presence of a maritime oriented socio-cultural matrix, largely characterized by a marginal socio-economic existence, where piracy is thinkable.

3   State "control" of "pirates" has relied on providing economic opportunity, and engendering a sense of personal loyalty to the state; and a state's failure to provide this leaves sea folk to fend for themselves, or seek patronage from alternative sources.

4   Patronage is important for any large scale organization of piracy.

5   There is a persistence of patron-client relationships.

6   Weak political development relative to economic expansion.

7   Piracy emerges during times of weak political control, when the state's political hegemony is challenged.

8   The complex physical and cultural geography limits the ability of the state to maintain rigid territorial boundaries. This was a particular concern for colonial states imposing their geopolitical consciousness on the region, and is problematic for the independent successors of those colonial states.

9   Regional and international co-operation is problematic due to competition for resources, and questions of sovereignty and territorial integrity.

10 A rough technological balance, inclusive of "tools" and "knowledge", is to the advantage of "pirates". When the state had a dramatic technological edge, virtually monopolizing access and use of technology *vis-à-vis* "pirates", such activities were largely brought under control.

11 Piracy is endemic to the maritime world of Southeast Asia, and will always exist in some form.

12 It is highly adaptive, finding the weak spots in state control.

---

proliferation of piracy in the nineteenth century should be seen as only a snapshot in time, without the benefit of being able to see the potential reconstitution of legitimate political structures, which had in the past resulted from the political and economic competition of raiding/piracy.

Into the latter half of the nineteenth century, the power dynamic in maritime Southeast Asia swung heavily toward Western colonial powers, and resulted in the imposition of Western political and legal systems. Although the shift had already happened earlier in European thinking, at this time piracy and raiding, indeed, all predatory maritime activities, became criminalized, illegitimate, outside society and imbued with Western concepts like *animo furundi* and *hostes humanis generis*. The entire suite of predatory maritime activities, legitimate and illegitimate, from the fifth to the nineteenth century, and extending to all such future activities, was indelibly linked to the Western term piracy and its subjective moral connotations. With the ascendancy of Western-style political and legal systems, "traditional" conceptions of piracy went into hiding, between the sinews of the new state structures, maintaining themselves where state control and influence did not reach.

One of the most pronounced and enduring changes was the state's conception of space and territory. Prior to the assertion of a Western geopolitical consciousness in the region, creating rigid territorial borders that needed to be maintained as part of the state's claim to legitimacy, territorial boundaries were much more flexible and porous. Territory was reckoned more by the extent of the rulers influence, where he could assert authority and control, rather than by prescribed, "permanent" boundaries.[70] Prior to the development of colonial states, the complex, fluid geography of maritime Southeast Asia, both physical and cultural, was not challenged. People used the seas as highways of trade and information exchange, linking regions together, more or less freely passing from one end of maritime Southeast Asia to the other. The compartmentalization of territory provided novel challenges to Western style states in controlling people's activities.

These dramatic conceptual shifts were accompanied by material and social change as well. Many sea folk, such as the Bajau Laut of Sempoerna District, Sabah, Malaysia,[71] readily adopted new technologies to improve their lifestyles. More importantly they also became involved in a monetized economy, radically changing old patterns of patron-client relations that had linked them to local power structures, with a ruler at the peak. Welcoming the break with traditional hierarchies, many engaged the new power structure, or at least the economic aspects of it, with enthusiasm. Social patterns shifted according to these changes, as sea folk adapted to the new socio-political-cultural reality. All of these changes created a drastically different environment in which contemporary piracy has emerged.

Thus in some ways, contemporary maritime piracy in Southeast Asia is very much a product of its time, specific to the rapidly globalizing, interconnected, high speed environment in which the world finds itself these days. Some "pirates" are using the latest technology, from machine guns to GPS and radar, to organize and carry out their attacks. Their networks are often extensive, taking advantage of advanced communications, modern transport, and electronic banking to facilitate their operations, which can involve "pirating" entire ships, cargo and crew. This is also combined with "lower level" piracy, sneak thieves, and/or robbers armed with knives and clubs, who do not have the resources to get the most advanced technology. Technical advancements, combined with rapid uneven economic develop characteristic of the last 30 years in Southeast Asia, culminating in the monetary crisis of 1997, has pushed piracy from the backwaters to the busiest sea-lanes in Southeast Asia, threatening local and international commercial traffic and the lives of their crews.

Efforts to combat piracy have been foiled by a lack of resources locally, economic turmoil, poor redistribution of wealth, and corruption. This failure of the state to effectively redistribute resources, exacerbated by the 1997 monetary crisis, has caused some sea folk to turn to piracy, and in some cases to seek alternative patrons and opportunities, such as those that have organized piracy into gangs and international syndicates. Local resources are severely strapped, but funding from international sources also has not been forthcoming,[72] despite the economic and military importance of Southeast Asian waterways. Additionally, attempts at addressing piracy through international law have been ineffective in Southeast Asia due to problems of definition, and due in part to the unwillingness of regional powers to co-operate. Thus the resurgence of piracy in the last 30 years is reflective of weak political development that has not kept pace with economic expansion, creating many factors which stimulate piracy, while at the same time handicapping the state's ability to respond to it. Thus piracy has resurfaced without effective controls, threatening the state's authority, and ultimately its legitimacy.

Despite the enormous changes between historical and contemporary piracy, there are many continuities of circumstance from which piracy has emerged, including continuities of practice, and continuities of the attempts of states to control "piracy." A similar cultural matrix exists today as existed 150 years ago, during the last high point of piracy. There is still a large group of maritime oriented, skilled, yet marginal and poor sea folk, who partake in a broad based subsistence strategy, much as there was in the past. And the modern state has not been able to fully "convert" them to its proscribed views of the world.

In the past, a vital component of a broad based survival strategy was raiding, as a way to take advantage of trade in the region that one might not otherwise have access to. Although criminalized, these practices remained "culturally thinkable", and provide a backdrop to potential rationalizations for acts of piracy today, whether to make ends meet for a poor fishermen, or for a petty criminal with no better way to make a buck.

To effectively control this population of sea folk, and thereby a large potential "labour pool" of piracy, states have, in the past and present, primarily relied on two methods to incorporate these people into the state structure: economic opportunity, and personal loyalty. In the past, economic opportunity was afforded by the state/ruler by controlling trade and effectively redistributing the wealth among the ruler's sea folk followers, a vital component of maritime state power structures. In addition to economic opportunity, the ruler could offer social prestige through title and rank, through association with the spiritually potent being of the ruler, or through oath taking and imprecation, establishing personal ties of loyalty. These connections were often durable, as was the case with the Orang Laut and the ruling line descendent from Srivijaya through Melaka, Riau, and Johor, exerting a powerful control over some sea folk. When these methods of control failed, as they did to quite a degree in the late eighteenth and early nineteenth centuries, circumstances of intense competition for authority and resources developed, thus setting the stage for an upsurge in piracy. Furthermore, with the shift of local power structures towards colonial domination, sea peoples increasingly found themselves and their traditional economic and political roles being marginalized, or becoming obsolete altogether, thereby cutting them off from participation in local and regional power structures.

Today, states still rely on similar forms of control to incorporate sea folk, and more broadly all their subjects, into the state, predominantly through economic aid, and extension of loyalties through national identity. State control of the rapid economic expansion over the last thirty years, despite real material gains in much of the region, has been uneven, leaving large pockets of people, particularly sea folk, in poverty and without access to economic opportunity. Although not the initial impetus for piracy, the monetary crisis in 1997 exacerbated the pre-existing inequalities, leading to further increases in piracy. This failure to effectively redistribute the wealth, and give sea folk a stake in the national economy, is made more important because the state has also not been able to initiate the personal relationships and mutual social obligations, provided in the past by a more personalized charismatic leadership.

Patrons of piracy, both today and historically, have provided key economic and organizational support for piracy/raiding: safe havens, markets, and capital. While not necessary for piracy to exist, these factors allow a greater scale of operation, as reflected by the large scale raids carried out historically with the support of legitimate political structures, and the high end hijackings of ships today. The relationships patrons engage in with their clients are part of a wide spread, flexible system of personalized power relations that permeate many of the state structures in the region, providing access to institutional support. The larger scale piracy engendered by patrons, likely incorporates many sea folk as labour, but also transcends their immediate concerns of escaping poverty, or making ends meet, broadening the scope of piracy as an end in itself. This scale of piracy (built in part upon the state's failure to control its people, and to provide basic support and opportunities for them) is a slightly different challenge to state control and state authority than the poverty of sea folk. This problem points out gaps in the state's ability to control non-state violence, and overtly challenges its political authority.

Piracy thrives in conditions of weak political control, and in itself further weakens that control, particularly in a contemporary setting. Historically, piracy could represent the dynamism of a society; the realignment of local power structures that could give rise to legitimate powers. Piracy could also represent the decay and fragmentation of power, as was the case for many Malay states in the nineteenth century. Today piracy only indicates weak state control, but in both instances, whether re-emergent or decaying political power, piracy develops in part out of a lack of political control.

Thus piracy is able to operate where political control is weak, so that the more widespread and egregious the attacks, the weaker and more extensive the lack of political control. Piracy emerges from gaps in political control, often created by other challenges to the political hegemony of the state, and then serves to widen those gaps, taking advantage of the state's reduced capacity to address piracy. Historically this can be seen clearly in the piracy associated with the Tay-son rebellion in Vietnam in the late eighteenth and early nineteenth centuries,[73] which created a rift in the political hegemony of Vietnam which then spilled over into Chinese waters. This rift, however, opened up because of pre-existing conditions of poverty, marginalization, and weak political control, and then expanded due to the states' preoccupation with other internal problems. Similarly, the Iranun took advantage of weakened political conditions in much of the archipelago (as well as growing Western trade with China), and their attacks served to further weaken regional political structures.

Today, the situation is not dissimilar. Uneven economic development and inability to incorporate sea folk into the state has created a background context in which piracy resurfaced, and recurrent challenges to political hegemony such as separatist movements in Aceh and the southern Philippines, corruption (facilitating the spread of influence that could be used to accommodate "piratical" activity), rogue elements of state apparatuses, and growing criminal networks, have made space for piracy to develop, and have drawn the attention of state security forces away from piracy itself. Political instability stemming from the monetary crisis, particularly in Indonesia, has further taxed state political authority.

A direct continuity with the past is the complex physical geography of Southeast Asia. Since rigid borders were imposed on the region in the nineteenth century, they have been highly contested or used to advantage by raiders/"pirates", smugglers, migrants, and traders. More challenges to these borders have arisen in the last few decades, such as economic and political refugees moving in massive waves through maritime Southeast Asia, and illegal fishing which costs billions in lost revenues.[74] These issues have become more difficult to deal with in the last 25 years, as a result of the 1982 UNCLOS having greatly expanded the amount of seascape that littoral states claim and for which they are responsible. Indeed, the expanding seascape under the jurisdiction of littoral states has stretched maritime security forces beyond their capabilities, particularly in the archipelagic states of Indonesia and the Philippines, as suggested by the persistence of piracy and unregulated population movements in these regions.

These borders are not only difficult to enforce due to the complex, fluid geography, but because they were also superimposed on the cultural geography of the region. The seas of Southeast Asia acted as convenient highways, connecting much of the archipelago in regional and international exchange networks. Migrations between historically linked areas, such as the Malay world centred on Sumatra, Malaysia, Borneo, and between modern Sabah, Malaysia, Sulu, and the rest of the southern Philippines, can be seen as an extension of these networks. The imposition of invisible boundaries in this environment has proven difficult to enforce, both for colonial states and contemporary states.

Loose political control is also evidenced by the inability of states to effectively co-operate to address the issue of piracy, and also by the priority that each individual state is able to accord piracy. Historically, colonial states in maritime Southeast Asia were generally not able to co-operate in addressing transnational threats like smuggling and piracy, until the latter half of the nineteenth century when their rivalry for territory and commerce had subsided or been for the most part, resolved. Similarly, in the past when states were beset by challenges to their political hegemony they were not able to prioritize piracy and effectively deal with it. Today, international co-operation amongst ASEAN members in dealing with piracy, and other transnational issues, has been fairly ineffective. Continuing rivalry over maritime boundary disputes, in part because of new claims to the seas stemming from the 1982 UNCLOS, and a general hypersensitivity to sovereignty issues (with several states still being actively engaged in establishing national identities), has made the addressing of piracy in a cooperative fashion problematic. Furthermore, individual states in the region, most notably Indonesia and the Philippines, but to some extent other littoral states as well, are not able to give piracy priority in their national agendas, despite rhetoric to the contrary.[75] Other internal and external challenges such as the Gerakan Aceh Merdeka (Aceh Independence Movement), West Papua, Moro Islamic Liberation Front, crime, corruption, poverty, illegal fishing, smuggling, and illegal immigration make piracy against other countries' ships a low priority . Thus it continues to increase with little effective opposition.

Thus controlling piracy is also problematized by threats to the political hegemony, stemming from a lack of international and regional co-operation, both historically and presently. In the past, regional powers, both local and European, had problems cooperating to curtail mutually worrisome piracy and raiding, largely due to competition over resources, including the flow of trade, and territory. This became particularly problematic when rigid territorial borders were erected, making their maintenance a primary concern, and thereby limiting cooperative efforts to address piracy if they would be seen as compromising territorial integrity, and/or control of vital resources. By the mid to late nineteenth century as competition for resources and territorial borders became more entrenched, colonial powers became more willing to co-operate. Similarly today, competition for natural resources, fish, oil, gas, and trade routes, is still of great importance, and still-emerging national identities, heavily reliant on a territorially defined nation, restrict Southeast Asian states' willingness to co-operate across borders, or accept direct foreign support. Possibly in the future, as in the past, when competition is less pronounced and state integrity is more certain, more effective regional co-operation may be possible.

The effect of technology on piracy is relatively simple when viewed in a dynamic continuum. When there is a relative balance in technology between those being called "pirates" and the state, as there was for much of the nineteenth century and as exists today, the advantage would seem to be in the favour of the "pirates". Controlling technology has become far more difficult in modern times. In the past the state had a virtual monopoly over advanced technology, as there was an immense imbalance between European technology and local technology in the nineteenth century. The playing field has largely been levelled today. Pirates have access to fire arms, boats, and information technology, commensurate with that of the state. Further, processes of globalization are extending information networks globally, and are largely beyond state control. The Internet, cell phones, modern transportation, and e-banking have created highly flexible systems of information organization that non-state actors are able to use effectively. "Pirates" with their greater flexibility, focused goals, tactics, and ability to "blend-in" make more effective use of technology than can the state. However, when and if the balance becomes heavily in the favour of the state, as happened in the later half of the nineteenth century, piracy, or at least its symptoms could be largely curtailed, or brought within acceptable limits.

Another component of technological advantage lies in superior knowledge. Historically, although piratical groups were technically "outgunned" by European powers, they had intimate local knowledge that allowed them to evade pursuit, and utilize hit and run tactics. Similarly today, although the pirates are making better use of available tools, the key is knowledge. Pirates increasingly know where, when and what to attack and how to "blend-in" and disappear. To suppress piracy, the state must know when and where "pirates" will attack, and know where their bases are, who are their patrons and where they are located. This was the key that allowed the Europeans to finally destroy the last raiding strong holds in maritime Southeast Asia. Thus states must be able to make more efficient use of the technology and available knowledge, because limiting "pirates" access is not likely to be feasible.

In the past piracy/raiding were intrinsic parts of the region, fundamental to state development, and a vital element of many regional cultures. Today piracy is not intrinsic, but is still very much endemic to maritime Southeast Asia. Although no longer imbued with the same societal significance as in the past, it is an inescapable part of this region. It has proven immensely adaptive to changing situations, and just as theft on land, no matter the moral rationale or justification behind it, no matter the advancements in surveillance and law enforcement, it will always exist. Since eliminating piracy is impossible, the task then is to limit its scope and operation, bringing its presence back under control, and making it an exception, not the rule.

A Way Forward

Contemporary piracy in Southeast Asia is a complex security threat that needs to be addressed. Yet, its complex nature has problematized efforts to combat piracy, particularly when approaches are not contextualized to maritime Southeast Asia. Overarching, broad approaches, like UNCLOS, used to combat piracy have been problematic in their application. Both conventions do not contextualize their approaches to maritime Southeast Asia, where the majority of incidents happen. More locally contextualized approaches need to be developed. There also needs to be established a clear understanding that long term responses should focus on the underlying causes, i.e., the roots of contemporary maritime piracy, while not ignoring the symptoms, i.e., the immediate threats to maritime security. In addressing both short term and long term security approaches to piracy, local capacity building needs to be emphasized.

To deal with the actual incidents of piracy themselves, local patrol capacities need to be developed, particularly in Indonesia and the Philippines, to address the threat they pose to life, property, and political authority. International funds, training, and materials need to be provided for these states to develop national coast guards,[76] or equivalent civil security forces, separate from military structures. The latter should be focused on addressing larger scale conflicts, not police functions. This also makes sense in terms of the ships needed to effectively combat piracy. Navies tend to focus budgets on purchasing large ships meant for national level defence, such as submarines, frigates, missile boats etc., where as what is most needed for anti-piracy efforts are small, fast patrol vessels able to outrun pirate speed boats, and pursue them into shallow coastal waters.[77] Coast guards would also help avoid concerns of regional co-operation, as they are not as threatening to sovereignty as are international security forces like the national military. Currently Japan is one of the very few states outside the region engaged in such capacity building, and yet they are certainly not alone in the benefits they derive from the strategic waters of Southeast Asia.

Regional co-operation is an area that bridges short term and long term approaches to controlling piracy. It is important to both, but as in the past, it is problematic in practice. In an effort to control actual incidents, greater co-operation across national borders is needed, as "pirates" do not respect the national maritime borders of littoral states in the region, and indeed actively exploit them. Previous commitments to regional co-operation have been largely ineffective, and lack key practical measures, such as provisions for active hot pursuit across borders. Despite growing awareness of the problem and the threat it poses, there is little more than vocal acknowledgement. Recent Singaporean co-operation with Japan, as well Japanese/Thai co-operation,[78] may signal, or stimulate, increasing willingness to co-operate on issues of transnational maritime security.[79] Regional anti-piracy agreements offer an interesting opportunity for regional co-operation, and could also avoid pitfalls of broader legal solutions by specifically targeting regional circumstances, and using local security forces.[80] To be effective in addressing maritime piracy, ASEAN should agree to broader regional co-operation, and taking the lead and not leaving it to foreign powers. Additionally, to be effective co-operation must have real teeth and take into account the complex nature of piracy in the region, addressing hit and run thugs as well as organized, transnational crime syndicates. Because knowledge has proven a critical aspect of combating piracy, information sharing could be a starting point for regional co-operation. Being able to infiltrate pirate organizations, and predict their next moves could be greatly facilitated by sharing relevant intelligence. This could eventually open the way for co-operation for pursuit and prosecution of pirates across national borders as well.

Despite the necessity of dealing with actual incidents of piracy, more emphasis needs to be placed on long term economic and political development of the region, as a way of addressing the circumstances that have produced this latest upsurge in piracy. Because of the strategic commercial and military interests in the waters of Southeast Asia, and the consistently high numbers of incidents of piracy in the region, international funds should be directed at encouraging sustainable[81] economic development and opportunities in littoral regions. Shipping companies in particular might take a leading role in this effort, as their interests are directly impacted by piracy.

Economic development, however, is not a panacea for piracy in itself. The economic development suggested would try to alleviate the most extreme and pervasive poverty among maritime populations, seeking to abrogate the motivation for turning to piracy. Economic development would also progressively incorporate maritime populations into the state, and give them a stake in maintaining legitimate power structures. These measures, however, would not directly address the motivations for hardcore piracy like ship hijackings, carried out by large criminal organizations, which can net millions of dollars. The motivation for these attacks is beyond what general economic development can directly address, but such incidents are also by far the minority. Economic development could, however, help dry up the large potential labour pool of pirates from which these organizations are likely recruiting. Additionally, reducing the number of recruits now could reduce the number of experienced, hardened pirates, responsible for brutal attacks like that involving the *Tenyu*. The entire crew of the *Tenyu* was clubbed to death and thrown overboard.[82] A steady, legitimate income could make the difference to many people for whom piracy is a thinkable option. Although much easier said than done, emphasis in this direction will help address the underlying problems rather than just the symptoms.

Political development also needs to accompany economic development; otherwise, any derived benefits will likely be squandered. More than simply trying to bail water, political development should seek to plug the holes where state control is leaking out. Part of this effort should be directed to including marginalized maritime populations in the identity of the state, thereby developing genuine loyalty and binding them to legitimate power structures. Indeed, the state needs to find a way to respectfully and positively include maritime peoples in the national identity, without ignoring local identities. Furthermore, corruption as an endemic practice needs to be limited, if not eliminated, so as to control the ability of illegitimate centres of power to operate within the state. At the same time, internal disputes that threaten further fragmentation of power need to be conscientiously addressed. Use of force while effective in the short run, is not very effective in garnering support of the nation. Moreover, it is seen as indicating a lack of ability to enforce the states will through other means.

Economic and political development are broad approaches to addressing piracy, and need to be tailored to more specific circumstances. One way this can be done is through researching the motivations of "pirates" through examining contemporary court, police, and prison records. These materials could also be supplemented by field research into maritime populations, looking at poverty, income sources, criminal networks, cultural continuity, and incorporation into state structures. Such research would provide insight that could help focus broader development strategies seeking to address maritime security in Southeast Asia.

The people of maritime Southeast Asia over the centuries have been both dynamic and flexible, adapting their survival strategies to the times. The roots of contemporary maritime piracy are long and deeply imbedded in the political and cultural traditions of the region. If they are to eventually be ripped out, regional states, with the support of the international community, need to enhance regional security by offering their peoples a viable alternative to piracy.

Notes

1   This chapter is based on a thesis submitted to the graduate division of the University of Hawaii in partial fulfilment of the requirements for the degree of Master of Arts in Asian Studies, May 2004.

2   Maritime security is rather self explanatory as security concerns related to the maritime realm, however, the other terms may not be as familiar. Grey area phenomenon is a term designating those security threats stemming from non-state actors that exist in the "gray areas" of states, where state control is not fully realized (Peter Chalk, *Non-Military Security and Global Order* (New York: St. Martin's Press, LLC, 2000), pp. 2–3). A "non-traditional security threat", as described in neo-realist security literature stemming from the Cold War, is a security threat that is not an immediate risk of causing full scale war between nations and therefore warranted less attention. Human security is a concept that has gained attention with the ending of the Cold War, which stimulated reexaminations of traditional security theory, such as the divide between traditional and non-traditional security threats, and "...refers to the quality of life of the people of a society or polity...[and] [a]nything that degrades their quality of life...is a security concern" (Ramesh Thakur, "Human Security Regimes", in *Asia's Emerging Regional Order*, edited by William T. Tow, Ramesh Chandra Thakur, and In-Taek Hyun (Tokyo, New York: United Nations University Press, 2000), p. 231).

3   This can be seen in articles such as that by P.W. Birnie, "Piracy: Past, Present and Future", *Marine Policy* 11 (July 1987): 163; where the opening paragraph links piracy from an indefinite historical past, to the middle ages, and to current day without contextualizing or providing any sense that piracy may have changed in those thousands of years. Similarly in William M. Carpenter, and David G. Wiencek, "Maritime Piracy in Asia", *Asian Security Handbook*, edited by William M. Carpenter, and David G. Wiencek (New York: Armonk, 2000), the opening paragraph links piracy as a threat from the earliest records of venturing to sea, to an upsurge in piracy in the 1970s and 1980s. Both of these articles are quite good, but they each fall prey to the temptation to make sweeping generalizations without any depth of analysis.

4   See, for instance, Philip A. Buhler, "New Struggle with an Old Menace: Towards a Revised Definition of Maritime Piracy", *International Trade Law Journal* (Winter, 1999), *LexisLaw* electronic printout 17p; Timothy H. Goodman, "Leaving the Corsair's Name to Other Times", *Case Western Reserve Journal of International Law* (Winter, 1999), *LexisLaw* electronic printout 24p; John Mo, "Options to Combat Piracy in Southeast Asia", *Ocean Development & International Law* 33, (2002): 343–58; among many others. These articles, and the many like them, are

quite good, but do not effectively contextualize the problem of piracy in Southeast Asia, where it is the most persistent. Other sources, such as James Warren, "A Tale of Two Centuries", ARI Working Thesis, no. 2, June 2003, <www.ari.nus.edu.sg/pub/wps.htm>; J.L. Anderson, "Piracy and World History: An Economic Perspective on Maritime Predation", *Journal of World History* 6, no. 2 (1995): 175–99, more effectively contextualize contemporary piracy.

[5]   See almost any historical work cited in this thesis for examples where disciplinary limits have necessarily cut off applying historical accounts to contemporary phenomena; it is simply outside the scope and aim of these works.

[6]   See in particular Ger Teitler, "Piracy in Southeast Asia: A Historical Comparison", *MAST* 1, no. 1 (2002): 67–83, available at <http://www.marecentre.nl/mast/httpwww.marecentre.nlmastmastnewvol1.1.html>; and Warren, 2003.

[7]   James Legge, *A Record of Buddhistic Kingdoms* (New York: Paragon Book Reprint Corp., Dover Publications, Inc., 1965), p. 112, Unaltered Republication of Oxford: Clarendon Press, 1886; and Paul Wheatley, *The Golden Khersonese* (Kuala Lumpur: University of Malay Press, 1961), p. 37.

[8]   Barbara Andaya, and Leonard Andaya, *A History of Malaysia* 2d ed. (Honolulu: University of Hawaii Press, 2001), pp. 26–27, 133; William Henry Scott, *Barangay* (Manila: Ateneo De Manila University Press, 1999), pp. 147–60; Warren, 2003, p. 3; Benedict Sandin, *The Sea Dayaks of Borneo* (Michigan State University Press, 1967), p. xv.

[9]   See Alfred P. Rubin, *The Law of Piracy* 2d ed. (New York: Transnational Publishers, Inc., 1998), for an in depth review of the varied uses of the word piracy over the last 2,000 years.

[10]   Joseph N.F.M. a Campo, "Discourse without Discussion: Representations of Piracy in Colonial Indonesia 1816–25", *Journal of Southeast Asian Studies* 34, no. 2 (June 2003), online print out: p. 2 of 20.

[11]   Ibid.

[12]   Rubin, p. 10.

[13]   Criminal in this sense defines actions punishable under local, municipal, or civil law, as opposed to necessitating recourse to international law or law governing war.

[14]   Meaning private motives, as opposed to political motives.

[15]   This phrase literally means "enemy of humankind", or "enemy to all humankind".

[16]   Rubin, p. 29.

[17]   Ibid., p. 39.

[18] Ibid., p. 93.

[19] Even today Article 101 of the United Nations Convention on the Law of the Sea (UNCLOS) defining piracy has a "private gains" stipulation, and Article 105 stipulating who may arrest "pirate vessels", states that "every State may seize a pirate ship or aircraft," affirming the principal of *hostes humani generis*.

[20] Rubin, p. 41, from Grotius, *De Jure Belli ac Pacis* Book II, ch. iii, para. 13(2).

[21] Ibid., p. 29.

[22] Monica Brito Vieira, "Mare Liberum vs. Mare Clausum," *Journal of the History of Ideas* 64, no. 3 (July 2003): 371.

[23] Kenneth J. Hagan, *This People's Navy* (New York: The Free Press, 1991), p. 63.

[24] William Edward Hall, *A Treatise on International Law* 8th ed., ed. A. Pearce Higgins (Oxford: Clarendon Press, 1924), pp. 620–21, in Janice E. Thomson, *Mercenaries, Pirates, and Sovereigns* (Princeton: Princeton University Press, 1994), p. 22.

[25] Ibid.

[26] The use of privateers in Europe was actually very similar to traditional states in Southeast Asia, which organized raiding expeditions from among their followers, and from which a share of profits was turned over to the ruler.

[27] Philip Gosse, *The History of Piracy* (New York: Tudor Publishing Company, 1934), p. 58.

[28] Daniel Defoe, *A General History of the Robberies and Murders of the Most Notorious Pyrates* (New York: Garland Publishing, 1972), Preface, A3.

[29] Thomson, p. 26.

[30] Anne Perotin-Dumon, "The Pirate and the Emperor" in *The Political Economy of Merchant Empires*, edited by James D. Tracy (Cambridge: Cambridge University Press, 1991), p. 222.

[31] *United Nations Convention of the Law of the Sea* (Montego Bay, Jamaica, 10 December 1982), <http://www.un.org/Depts/los/convention_agreements/texts/unclos/closindx.htm>.

[32] "Piracy and Armed Robbery Against Ships Annual Report", 1 January–31 December 2003, *Piracy Reporting Centre* (Kuala Lumpur: ICC International Maritime Bureau, 2003), p. 3.

[33] Wheatley, p. 37.

[34] Ibid., p. 38.

[35] Personal Communication, Pang Yong, 3 February 2004; and Personal Communication, Koh Keng We, 6 February 2004.

[36] Wheatley, pp. 47, 57.

[37] Jeffery Hayes, Personal Communication, 3 February 2004; and Koh Keng We, Personal Communication, 4 February 2003.

[38] Wheatley, p. 226.

39   Carl A. Trocki, *Prince of Pirates* (Singapore: Singapore University Press, 1979), p. 56.

40   *Encyclopedia of Asian History*, vol. 3, s.v. "Piracy in the Malay World", Carl A. Trocki.

41   Raja Ali Haji ibn Ahmad, *The Precious Gift: Tuhfat al-Nafis* trans. Virginia Matheson, and Barbara Watson-Andaya (Kuala Lumpur: Oxford University Press, 1982): 261–62.

42   Scott, pp. 156–57.

43   Barbara Andaya, "The Role of the Anak Raja", *Journal of Southeast Asian Studies* 7, no. 2 (1976): 167.

44   Timothy Barnard, "Multiple Centers of Authority" (Ph.D. dissertation, University of Hawaii at Manoa, 1998), p. 212.

45   Andi Zainal Abidin, *Sekali Lagi La Ma'dukelleng Arung Singkang* [Once Again La Ma'dukelleng Arung Sungkang] (Ujung Pandang: Panitia Dasa Warsa IKIP, 1975): 2, 9, 26.

46   Scott, p. 154.

47   Ahmad, pp. 264, 268.

48   Abdin, p. 12.

49   Nicholas Tarling, *Piracy and Politics in the Malay World* (Melbourne: F.W. Cheshire, 1963), p. 1.

50   See Defoe, 1972 for various descriptions of the wretched forced to piracy or those that openly chose the path. See as well C. Whitehead Esq., *Lives and Exploits of English Highwaymen, Pirates and Robbers* (London: Charles Daly, 19, Red Lion Square, Holborn, 1839) for similar descriptions of pirates.

51   Tarling, p. 8. Also see Trocki, 1979, for a good account of the political developments of the late eighteenth and nineteenth century in the Malay world, especially emphasizing local political developments rather than emphasizing European policy as Tarling does.

52   For example, UNCLOS's definition of piracy that stipulates private gains, international waters, and the use of boats, is problematic in Southeast Asia.

53   Rubin, pp. 2–3.

54   Tarling, 1963, p. 1.

55   Campo, pp. 1–2 of 20.

56   In particular see the works of James Warren on Sulu, the Iranun and the Balangingi, the thoughtful article by N.F.M. a Campo on the discourse of piracy, the works of history by Barbara and Leonard Andaya, Dian Murray's work on piracy in southern China, Rubin's work on the law of piracy, and Janice Thomson's look at piracy in European state formation, among others cited in this chapter.

57   Edward Said, *Orientalism* (New York: Vintage Books, 1978), p. 10.

58 Adam Young and Mark J. Valencia, "Conflation of Piracy and Terrorism in Southeast Asia: Rectitude and Utility", *Contemporary Southeast Asia* 25, no. 19 (2003): 272.

59 Leslie Green, *The Authority of the State* (Oxford: Clarendon Press, 1988), pp. 1, 79.

60 Thomson, pp. 8, 41–42, 54.

61 Ibid., p. 54.

62 Muthiah Alagappa, "Introduction", in *Political Legitimacy in Southeast Asia*, edited by Muthiah Alagappa (Stanford: Stanford University Press, 1995), p. 2; Micheal Leifer, *Dilemmas of Statehood in Southeast Asia* (Vancouver: University of British Columbia Press, 1972), 105; Green, p. 1.

63 Alagappa, p. 3.

64 Andaya and Andaya, p. 58.

65 See Trocki, pp. 45, 47, 55 for discussion of the British founding of Singapore in co-operation with the Temmenggong Abdul Rahman, among others, and see also Andaya, and Andaya, pp. 134–35; as well as Ahmad, pp. 261–64, mentioning Dutch-Riau co-operation to destroy an Iranun base near Retih.

66 Andaya and Andaya, p. 118.

67 Rubin, pp. 217–18.

68 As may be seen from the Battle of *Beting Marau*, one of the largest "anti-piracy" missions in the Malay world, where James Brooke in command of a composite force of British warships and Iban prahus, decimated a rival contingent of Iban raiders, or "pirates" as Brooke saw them, which did not happen until July of 1849 (Pringle, p. 81). Likewise, Spanish attacks on the home bases of Iranun and Balangingi in the Sulu archipelago were not carried out until the 1840s, and again in the 1860s, when steamships made these attacks possible.

69 Eric Tagliacozzo, "Kettle on a Slow Boil: Batavia's Threat Perceptions in the Indies Outer Islands, 1870–1910", *Journal of Southeast Asian Studies* 31, no. 1 (March 2000), p. 74.

70 For a good discussion of this notion of flexible power see the influential work O.W. Wolters, *History, Culture, and Region in Southeast Asian Perspectives* Southeast Asia Programme Publications, no. 26 revised (Ithaca: Cornell Southeast Asia Programmes Publications, 1999).

71 For a detailed discussion of the Bajau Laut see for example Clifford Sather, *The Bajau Laut* (Kuala Lumpur: Oxford University Press, 1997).

72 With the notable exception of Japan, which has contributed materially in the form of money and ships as well as providing training.

73 For a detailed discussion of piracy in this region and time see Dian Murray, *Pirates of the South China Coast 1790–1810* (Stanford: Stanford University Press, 1987).

74 "Indonesia's Losses from Foreign Fish Poachers Down 50 Pct", *Asia Pulse*, 24 September 2003, sec. Northern Regional Territory.

75 Mo, p. 348

76 See Sam Bateman, "Coast Guards: New Forces For Regional Order and Security", East West Center Asia Pacific Issues, no. 65 (Honolulu: Sales Office East West Center, January 2003), for a good discussion of the potential value of developing coast guards in the Asia-Pacific region.

77 Chalk, 1997, p. 96.

78 See Donald Urquhart, "Japan to hold anti-piracy drills with Thailand", *Business Times Singapore*, 26 February 2004, sec. Shipping Times.

79 This most recent spate of co-operative exercises with Japan could also be part of a broader political cat and mouse game, as Southeast Asian countries try to court both China and Japan, in an effort to balance these dominant political and economic rivals against each other.

80 Goodman, p. 5 of 24.

81 This term is variously defined, but here simply refers to the capacity for local reproduction of economic development, and the ability of local groups to be able to take advantage of development by legitimate means.

82 "South Sea Piracy", *The Economist*, 18 December 1999, U.S. Edition.

2

The Scourge of Piracy in Southeast Asia: Can Any Improvements be Expected in the Near Future?

P. Mukundan

Introduction

This chapter is an overview of the key current issues and trends in piracy, with a focus on Southeast Asia. It takes the perspective of the International Maritime Bureau (IMB) and the commercial interests it represents.

There are a number of worrying trends in piracy. Some of these are clear from statistics on piracy, which indicate increasing numbers of pirate attacks. Yet numbers do not tell the whole story. There are a number of other changes that have taken place in the area of piracy recently, some of which are hopeful. After outlining a general typology of pirate attacks and presenting a statistical overview, the paper will endeavour to shed light on some of these changes. The final section of the paper highlights the proactive role of the IMB in combating piracy.

For the purposes of this paper, the term *piracy* includes "piracy" as defined under article 101 of UNCLOS and "armed attacks" as defined by the MSC/Circ.984 of the IMO and *pirates* as those involved in perpetrating such attacks.

Types of Attacks

The IMB Piracy Reporting Centre (IMB-PRC) collates reports of piracy against vessels whether in port or on the high seas. These reports cover a wide spectrum of attacks.

At one end of the spectrum are the opportunistic attacks, or "maritime muggings". A group of pirates board a vessel with the intention of stealing whatever they can. The favourite targets are money in the Captain's safe, crew's personal valuables, and ship's equipment and stores within easy reach.

Petty theft of this kind is not new. It used to be the case that such pirates were easily frightened off by the crew. What differentiates contemporary attacks is that the pirates are better armed, expect greater returns, and are more determined. If they are able to enter the accommodation, crew's valuables or bridge equipment not locked away might be stolen. Many of the pirates head for the safe in the Captain's cabin and are quite prepared to injure or kill the Captain and crew if they cannot get what they want.

At the other end of the spectrum is the hijacking and theft of a vessel and her cargo. These crimes are planned well in advance with ships deliberately targeted usually for the value and easy disposal of the cargo. In most cases, the value of the ship and the cargo each amounts to millions of dollars. Attacks involve highly trained pirate gangs armed with knives and automatic weapons boarding the vessel with false ship's papers, cargo papers, and passports. These pirates are capable of operating the vessel without the crew's assistance. Violence and intimidation of the crew are invariably a feature of such attacks. In a few cases, like those of the Cheongson and Tenyu in 1998, whole crews have been murdered (see IMB Annual Piracy Report 1998).

Vessels are also hijacked for the primary purpose of abducting the crew for ransom. This is discussed in more detail in the ensuing sections.

In between these two extremes of petty theft and hijacking, the vast majority of attacks involve varying degrees of violence and audacity.

The Numbers

The best comparision of figures over the years are the annual numbers. The IMB-PRC recorded a total of 445 attacks in 2003 as opposed to 370 attacks on vessels in 2002. These range from attacks against vessels in port or at anchor, theft of stores and equipment from vessels, to the hijacking of ships and theft of shiploads of cargo.

In 2003 three quarters of the total number of incidents were from the countries as shown in Table 2.1.

In 2002 the IMB-PRC recorded 25 hijackings. This is unacceptably high. One hundred and ninety-one crew were taken hostage (of which 77 in Indonesia and 47 in Somalia), 38 crew were injured, 10 killed, and 24 missing. Guns were used in 68 attacks and knives in 136 attacks.

In 2003 the IMB-PRC recorded 445 attacks. During this year 19 vessels were hijacked, 359 crew or passengers were taken hostage, and 21 of these were killed. Attacks with guns and knives amounted to a total of 243 attacks, again the highest so far in a twelve-month period. Indonesia continues to account for approximately 27 per cent of all attacks worldwide.

TABLE 2.1
Incidents of piracy by country, 2002 and 2003

Country	2002	2003
Indonesia	103	121
Bangladesh	32	58
India	18	27
Malacca Straits	16	28
Malaysia	14	–
Nigeria	14	39
Vietnam	12	15
Guyana	12	–
Ecuador	12	–
Gulf of Aden/Red Sea	11	18
Venezuela	8	13
Philippines	10	12

Analysis of Current Factors Influencing Piracy

The ISPS Code

At the time of writing, the International Ship and Port facility Code (ISPS) Code was planned to come into effect on 1 July 2004. The ISPS was introduced by the IMO in 2002 to introduce a security regime to make ships and ports more secure in the light of the terrorist threat. This has put security planning and response on ships and in ports on a formal basis. If this is implemented in the spirit as in the letter, it must lead to an improvement in the security situation and hence in the incidents of piracy. There are over 55,000 vessels and many tens of thousands of ports which have to be brought to the required standard by 1 July 2004. A significant portion of this number has not begun planning for compliance with the Code yet. As July 2004 draws closer, it may happen that compliance with the Code in some parts of the world will degenerate into a box-ticking exercise to comply with the documentary requirements. So whilst the ISPS Code will bring about better security in many parts of the world, there will be other areas where major security vulnerabilities exist, covered by a fig leaf of documentary compliance.

Hijackings

Prior to 2001, the majority of hijackings were against merchant ships, aimed at the theft of the ship and the cargo. A significant change now is that there are very few cases of merchant ships being hijacked for this purpose. The reason for this is probably the fact that most vessels hijacked in this way have been recovered — in many cases with the pirate crew on board and the cargo partially or wholly intact. Pirates have been convicted in India and China and have received severe sentences.

On the other hand, a gang of pirates in Indonesia was recently convicted and many of them sentenced to two years imprisonment for hijacking an Indonesian vessel in Indonesian waters, with Indonesian crewmembers carrying an Indonesian cargo. The crew were abandoned on an uninhabited island by the hijackers. There are many who felt that this was a derisory punishment for such a serious crime and does nothing to deter pirates from their trade. There is in fact another gang of hijackers awaiting trial in Indonesia for the hijacking of the tanker Selayang. Let us hope that this will not be another opportunity missed by the judicial authorities.

Nevertheless, the seizure of these vessels and the pirates has tilted the risk/reward balance against the pirate gangs who invest funds upfront in the hope of the rewards which later flow from the sale of the cargo.

Overall, the response against these kinds of attacks have been successful and this kind of hijacking has been brought under control — for the moment.

Hijacking gangs have moved their attention to the softer targets presented by tugs and barges. These vulnerable vessels are lucrative targets. Barges typically carry 3000 tonnes of palm oil products, timber, or other easily disposable cargo.

Another form of current hijacking is where crewmembers are removed from the vessel and a ransom demanded for their return. Crew have been abducted for ransom for many years by militia groups in the Southern Philippines. On 10 August 2003, the Malaysian tanker Penrider was hijacked by eight armed pirates bound for Penang inside the Northbound Traffic Separation Scheme in the Malacca Straits. The Master was ordered to cross the Traffic Separation Scheme towards Indonesia. The pirates eventually left the vessel, taking with them the Master, Chief Engineer and Greaser and demanded a ransom for their return. Over the next days, the kidnapped crew were transferred from fishing vessel to fishing vessel at sea, whilst the negotiations continued. After agreement was reached on the ransom, they were released. Previous cases of abduction of crew from vessels in Northern Malacca Straits have been associated with the separatist GAM rebels in Aceh. Certain aspects of the Penrider case appeared to indicate that this operation could have been conducted by criminals posing as GAM rebels.

Violence

There is a danger in reading too much into the exact figures in any set of statistics. Crime statistics are underreported, particularly in the case of piracy. What is perhaps more important are overall trends and ballpark levels. It is important to treat figures with a dose of sound common sense to avoid descending into a purely theoretical, and perhaps irrelevant, analysis of the problem. For example, the 21 persons killed in 2003 compared to the 10 persons killed in 2002 represents a more than a 50 per cent increase in 2003. But as the levels of deaths in previous years have generally been in the twenties, this does not represent the shocking escalation that might appear from just looking at the numbers over two years. Also, it is important to consider deaths along with numbers of crew reported missing for a proper understanding of this grim statistic.

There have been more attacks using guns and knives than in previous years. This is probably a reflection of the greater availability and use of weapons in the countries with piracy problems. The number of crew/ passengers taken hostage has in recent years been around 200. In 2003 it was 359, which represents a significant increase. As noted in section 3 above, the number of crew killed and injured has risen. Indonesia, Nigeria, and Bangladesh are the areas with the highest levels of armed attacks. It is safe to conclude that the levels of violence used in these attacks are high and show no sign at present of dropping.

Types of Vessels

In 2003, tankers accounted for a greater number of attacks than previously. Whilst most of the tankers attacked in Southeast Asia are small chemical and product tankers, larger tankers have also been attacked. The obvious reason for this could be that fully laden tankers have a low freeboard and are easier to board. Tankers have small crews on board, there are fewer places for the crew to hide, and the product oil cargoes of fuel and gas oil are easy to dispose of. Whatever the reason for the boarding, one cannot ignore the danger of these vulnerable vessels in the hands of unauthorized and inexperienced attackers, whose primary concern is not the safety of the vessel.

Co-operation

When the piracy statistics were first compiled by the IMB-PRC in 1992, many countries in Asia refused to accept that they had a piracy problem. At that time, from their perspective this was correct. Few cases were reported to law enforcement agencies and piracy did not feature within their priorities. Many vessels suffered attacks, knew of no place to report them, and continued on their voyage. Some vessels which did report attacks were subjected to lengthy delays whilst police investigated and took statements from the crew. In a few notable cases, rather than investigating the case, the crew were themselves accused by law enforcement officers of murder and smuggling. This and the fact that the industry saw no real results, such as the arrest and prosecution of the pirates, hindered proper reporting of these incidents.

Today, over ten years later, the situation is different. There is great awareness by governments and law enforcement agencies of the problems of piracy. There is a much greater willingness to discuss these matters openly and to work together regionally to try and solve them. A number of initiatives are currently underway. There is better co-operation between law enforcement agencies. In many of the serious cases, it has been the experience of the IMB-PRC, that law enforcement agencies will act swiftly to stop and inspect a suspected hijacked vessel or phantom ship — a response the industry could not have envisaged in the early nineties. The recovery of vessels such as the Siam Xanxai, Petro Ranger, Global Mars, Alondra Rainbow, Selayang, Inabukwa, and many others are evidence of this. Credit for these cases must go the law enforcement agencies which understood how this crime works, which understand the limitations of ship registration and identity documents, and which acted quickly to seize the vessel.

How Can Technology Help?

The ISPS Code has made ship managers and operators more open to the idea of using technology to improve security. There are a number of technological devices and systems which are on the market or being developed to assist in securing the vessels better. For cost and other practical reasons, many of these may not make it in a cost conscious shipping environment.

When the ISPS Code is implemented in mid 2004 the Ship Alert and Automated Identification System (AIS) systems will become standard equipment on vessels. This paper does not deal in detail with these systems (for more information refer to the ISPS Code). Whilst Ship Alert may assist in limiting the kind of attacks discussed in this paper, it is debatable whether AIS will bring about a reduction in piracy attacks.

The following are two systems which the IMB recommends and are currently in use. Information on these systems may be obtained from <www.shiploc.com> and <www.secure-marine.com>.

SHIPLOC: Tracking System to Locate Hijacked Vessels

It is difficult to avoid hijackings of vessels. The vessels are usually targeted well in advance and are attacked by heavily armed and ruthless pirates. One of the best ways to counter such crimes is to have a tracking device on board which secretly transmits the vessel's position.

The IMB has been working together with *CLS*, a world leading satellite tracking system operator, to produce a satellite tracking system called SHIPLOC. SHIPLOC has been specially designed to locate ships at sea or in port and has already been installed on a great many ships.

The tiny transmitter is relatively inexpensive and can be concealed onboard ships. For their own safety, the crew of the ship need not be informed of the existence or location of the transmitter. SHIPLOC enables the ship owners to monitor the exact location of their ships. The only equipment needed is a PC with Internet access. In addition to its value if the vessel is hijacked, SHIPLOC facilitates independent and precise location of the vessel by its manager ashore as part of daily operations. SHIPLOC now complies with the requirements of the ISPS Code. The efficacy of SHIPLOC was made clear in the recovery of the hijacked tanker Selayang in June 2001 (See IMB Annual Piracy Report 2001). There are a number of other tracking devices also on the market. The IMB strongly encourages ship owners to install a tracking device of some kind on board their ships.

SECURE-SHIP: The Anti-Boarding System

Secure Marine in the Netherlands has developed a unique preventive and deterrence system to combat piracy. Secure-Ship is a non-lethal, electrified fence surrounding the ship which has been specially adapted for maritime use.

The fence uses a 9000-volt current to deter boarding attempts. If the fence is tampered with, an alarm will go off, activating floodlights and a very loud siren. The fence is collapsible, enabling quick installation and dismantling. Special quick release gates are used in case a pilot wants to board, for lowering a gangway or for launching a life raft. A smart control system enables remote operation. The fence has been tested at various sea conditions up to Beaufort force 7 without giving out false alarms. For safety reasons it cannot be used on tankers, gas carriers, or other vessels carrying inflammable cargoes.

The Role of the IMB Piracy Reporting Centre (IMB-PRC)

The IMB-PRC was set up in 1992 at the request of ship owners who wanted a centre to which attacks against ships could be reported and passed on to law enforcement agencies without incurring delays to the vessel. Today it provides the most comprehensive, contemporaneous information on attacks against ships worldwide, accounting for 95 per cent or more of the statistics published by the IMO. Its reports are considered by policy makers and law enforcement agencies. It remains the *only single point* for Masters to report attacks wherever they may be in the world.

Its piracy information services are free of charge to ship owners and Masters at all times. It is funded by donations from the industry and the ICC International Maritime Bureau.

The IMB-PRC receives reports of pirate attacks from the frontline victims of this crime, the Masters of vessels. This information is collated and broadcast to shipping in all the world's piracy hotspots around 00:00 hours UTC through the Inmarsat SafetyNet system. The daily broadcast provides vital information to the Masters of the location and type of recent attacks so that he or she can be better prepared as the vessel transits these areas.

The reports of the attacks are promptly passed to the nearest law enforcement agency for their information and action. The IMB-PRC also provides advice on trends and gives precise information on piracy attacks in current hotspots to law enforcement agencies, thus enabling the optimum deployment of law enforcement units. This has successfully resulted in the reduction of attacks, from time to time, in places like the Gelasa Straits, Bintan Islands, and in parts of the Indonesian Malacca Straits.

Weekly reports of attacks are placed on the IMB website <www.icc-ccs.org> every Tuesday. Quarterly and annual reports are prepared of attacks against vessels with a detailed breakdown of location of the attacks, types of attacks, type of arms used, type of vessels attacked, number of attempted and actual attacks, number and geographical location of vessels attacked at anchor, and whether they are steaming or berthed.

The IMB-PRC investigates hijacking of vessels and works closely with law enforcement agencies towards their recovery. Confidential information from IMB informants has led to the recovery of a number of hijacked vessels including the Global Mars, Anna Sierra, Al-Hufoof, and the Han Wei.

The collation of information on piracy attacks is important to understanding the scale of the problem and devising response strategies. It is submitted that the body collating this information should be independent from governments and law enforcement agencies that are charged with responding to piracy. Over the years the IMB has occasionally come under pressure by governments to water down the statistics or change definitions to meet the requirements of the day. The governments making these demands have often been those highlighted as having piracy hot spots. It is because the IMB represents business and is not dependent upon governments for finances or otherwise, that these pressures have been successfully resisted.

It is vital as we move into 2004 and beyond, that the collection of primary information on piracy remains independent and in the business sector. Masters and ship owners should feel comfortable reporting to and receiving advice from such a centre without fear of political interference.

Conclusions

The number of piracy attacks is up. Violence used in the attacks has increased. Attacks against tankers have increased. The potential danger of these vulnerable vessels with volatile cargoes in the hands of pirates or other unauthorized groups is a matter of some concern.

There have been successes. The hijacking of vessels for the theft of the shipload of cargo has reduced dramatically. This is largely because many of these vessels and often their cargoes have been recovered, thanks to the efforts of law enforcement agencies working closely with each other and with the IMB Piracy Reporting Centre.

The implementation of the ISPS Code should improve security overall. It is however important that as pressure mounts to comply by 1 July 2004, it does not become a paper exercise.

More shipping companies are prepared to look at technological devices which might help security. But it will only be those devices seen as cost effective that will be widely used.

The collation of primary information on attacks is critical to formulating responses. The reporting of incidents should be made as easy as possible for Masters of ships. It is submitted that the function of receiving information from Masters should be business sponsored, independent of government agencies charged with responding to incidents.

There is much greater awareness of piracy and exchange of information today among government agencies in Asia than ever before. We need to build on these strengths to deal with the challenges of tomorrow which, in addition to piracy, include other maritime crimes such as mass illegal immigration, smuggling, and the threat of maritime terrorism.

3

Ships Can Be Dangerous, Too: Coupling Piracy and Terrorism in Southeast Asia's Maritime Security Framework[1]

Graham Gerard Ong

Introduction

Piracy continues to be an enormous problem in Southeast Asia especially in Indonesian waters and along the Straits of Malacca and Singapore, which serves as the jugular of maritime trade in this region. There is no alternative to an efficient and viable route through maritime Southeast Asia other than to traverse between the Indian and Pacific Oceans. One of the most important international shipping routes from the Indian Ocean to the South China Sea (which conjoins with the Pacific Ocean) passes through the Straits of Malacca and Singapore. Eighty per cent of Japan's oil passes through the Malacca Straits. Indeed, 60 per cent of Australia's traffic goes through the adjacent Indonesian waters.[2] Singapore's harbour, as the world's busiest transit port, sits on the straits as a key hub in the global economic lifeline.

What is more disturbing is the escalation of piracy towards greater violence, to the point where the word "terror" has become increasingly invoked. In the last few years, maritime terrorism — acts of terrorism targeting ships at port or sea as well as ports themselves — has been added as another threat to Southeast Asia's maritime security. While no actual acts of maritime terrorism have been carried out as yet, intelligence analysts believe that regional terrorist networks will instinctively target the region's maritime infrastructure, "the soft belly...that can be attacked with little effort".[3] Consequently, while valid arguments can be made against the claim that a "nexus" exists between these two threats to maritime security — in the sense that terrorists and pirates conspire together in achieving their separate objectives — "in the charged political atmosphere, the mass media and governments have blurred the line between piracy and acts of terrorism."[4]

Indeed, this sentiment was exemplified in one of the suggestions made by Singapore's Minister for Defence Professor Tony Tan during a session on maritime security in the recent Asia Security Conference organized by the London-based International Institute for Strategic Studies held in Singapore in June 2003:

> We have been dealing with the problem of piracy for some time, and there are methods and tactics associated with terrorism which we can identify, and put in place several preventive measures.[5]

Singapore's Home Affairs Minister Wong Kan Seng put the issue more clearly in a media interview in December 2003:

> If there's a crime conducted at sea, sometimes we do not know whether it's pirates or terrorists who occupy the ship so we have to treat them all alike...So in other words if it's piracy we treat it just like terrorism because it is difficult to identify the culprits concerned unless you board the ship.[6]

Minister Wong also reaffirmed Minister Tan's earlier remark that countries in the region should "build on regional anti-piracy frameworks that already exist or are starting to come into place".[7]

This article builds on this proposition and explores how the threat of maritime terrorism can be "coupled" with piracy within Southeast Asia's maritime security framework. *Inter alia*, the purpose of such a project would be to sharpen the attention on piracy, which is a relatively neglected concern by regional governments as compared to the threat of terrorism that has recently besieged the security of most states. At the same time, the implications of piracy in the waters of the Malacca Straits clearly reflects the stark consequences that an act of maritime terrorism can have in the region.

The Virulent Turn within Piracy in Southeast Asia

The general magnitude of pirate attacks against the world's shipping remains unchanged since the new millennium. According to the International Maritime Bureau's (IMB) 2000 Annual Report, the number of reported incidents of piracy in 2000 stood at 469. This is an increase of 56 per cent over 1999 and quadruple the number of incidents in 1991.[8] In IMB's latest report, Piracy and Armed Robbery Against Ships, released in July 2003, 234 attacks were reported in the first half of the year. Assuming that the trajectory of attacks continues, the number of reported incidents for the year 2003 would be about the same as 2000.[9] Still, the number of attacks in the first six months of this year presents a 37 per cent increase over the 171 reported incidents in the corresponding period in 2002.[10]

As in 2000, the indications of the latest IMB report will place Southeast Asia as the most dangerous region for piracy in the world. Indonesia, for one, continues to possess the most piracy-prone waters after the Malacca Straits. There were 64 incidents in the first six months of 2003. At this current trajectory by the year's end, Indonesia will have maintained its 25 per cent share of the world's total reported attacks reported in 2000.[11] Conversely, the number of attacks in the Malacca Straits has gone down over the first six months of 2003. As a piracy analyst rightly inferred, "[the pirates] seem to have gone deeper into Indonesian waters".[12] Right up to March 2003, an attack was reported almost daily along the Gaspar Strait which is the vital waterway between the Indonesian islands of Bangka and Belitung and the fastest route for ships heading from Singapore to Jakarta or western Australia.[13]

However, unlike the maritime states in the region which are known to jealously guard their maritime boundaries, pirates are outlaws who do not recognize the interstate borders sanctioned by international law and treaties. Thus, pirates can return to the waters surrounding the Malacca Straits when security is lacking, just as easily as they have withdrawn into the internal waters of Indonesia. In tandem with the latest warning by the IMB to stay away from the Indonesian islands of Anambas and Bintan, the Bureau also cautions against "anchoring along the Indonesian coast of the [Malacca Straits] unless required for urgent operational reasons."[14]

What is most disturbing about piracy worldwide, and Southeast Asia in particular, is the fact that the attacks are becoming increasingly violent.[15] Attackers are more likely to be armed, and crewmembers are more likely to be killed or injured during attacks.[16] As Chalk has indicated, "Since the end of the Cold War, there has been a quantum leap in the violence potential threshold of pirates and other sub-state insurgents, who are now able to take advantage of a huge array of sophisticated weaponry left over from wars in Afghanistan and Cambodia as well as the former Red Army — much of it available at "bargain basement prices".[17] By extension, the employment of light arms such as automatic rifles and pistols (or the attempt to use them) while small in nominal terms has nearly tripled since 2000.[18]

For the first six months of 2003, Indonesia and the Malacca Straits collectively rank first for incidents of piracy involving the use of guns (34.5 per cent of the total). These areas also still collectively rank first for incidents involving the use of knives (31.2 per cent of the total) and for incidents involving "other weapons" (23 per cent of the total).[19] In the same six months, Indonesia and the Malacca Straits again rank first for incidents of piracy involving hostage taking and crew members being threatened with violence; second for incidents involving physical assaults and injury of crew members; and third for deaths inflicted.[20]

Another disturbing trend in maritime Southeast Asia is the rise of hijackings among incidents of piracy in the last few years.[21] From January to November 2002, there were 20 hijackings along the Malacca Straits alone.[22] Thus, it is becoming harder to accept the "*short term* seizure of vessels and acts of robbery, vandalism, threats of violence against the crew if demands are not met, or *in some cases,* acts of violence" as the mainstay of maritime Southeast Asia.[23] The current trend in hijacking now points towards extended seizure. An increasing number of cases are pushing the notion of "threats" and "acts of violence" by pirates towards the norm rather than the exception.

Both the employment of weapons by pirates and the increase in hijacking have vast consequences for the safety of life at sea and for international maritime navigation, especially along the Malacca Straits. The reason is clear. The Malacca Straits is the world's busiest waterway of 500 nautical miles in length and which gives passage to more than half the world's commerce at a rate of between 150 to as much as 900 ships daily.[24] It is extremely narrow especially along its southern half where it is about 20 nautical miles wide and only 9 nautical miles wide at the southern end. Such attacks against a steaming ship will not only put the lives of its crew at risk but also threaten the safe passage of other vessels and the lives of their crew through a massive collision. The disruption of maritime traffic along the Straits will interrupt (and even cripple) regional and international trade. As a latest example, on 13 August 2003, a 3,000 tonne Taiwanese fishing trawler in the Malacca Straits was strafed with rapid gunfire by two pursuing pirate boats resulting in the wounding of its captain, as well as the crippling of its bridge steering area and radar and communication equipment.

Hence, with the embellishment of what one could call "extreme acts of piracy", it is has become increasingly difficult to solely defer to the label "pirate". For example, the New York Times attributed a series of attacks on chemical tankers in the Malacca Straits involving the use of automatic weapons by the assailants — some ships were sprayed with bullets-in March 2003 to the work of "terrorists". However, it was later revealed that the pirates were only after valuables and equipment. "In other words, they were pirates, albeit unusually bold and violent ones."[25]

The Turn towards Maritime Terrorism in Southeast Asia

As with piracy, terrorism or "political terrorism" as it is sometimes labelled, is not new to Southeast Asia.[26] During the Cold War and even during the first half of the 1990s, terrorism was associated with two types of activities that have plagued much of the post-colonial history of the region. These include communist organizations — which have subsided since the end of the Cold War — and armed separatist movements-which persist till today — both which have carried out violent assaults against the government and civilians, including terrorist attacks. While it is true that the current terrorist threat posed by radical Islamic groups such as the Abu Sayyaf in the Philippines have been in existence since the 1990s, the international connection between Muslim extremism and other foreign Islamic organizations only surfaced in 1995 following the capture of a terrorist residing in the Philippines who had links to the radical Egyptian group Gama'a el Islamiyah (the alleged mastermind of the 1993 World Trade Centre bombing).[27]

Still, "though provoking international concern through widespread violence, domestic terrorists and their vision of establishing independent states appeared to pose little threat to global order and security". The international complicity between regional groups was only taken seriously after Osama bin Laden's al-Qaida organization made its existence and cause explicit through the attacks in Washington and New York on 11 September 2001.[28] "The events of Sept[ember] 11 were thus as much a wake-up call to Southeast Asia as they were to the United States and its traditional allies. Authorities are now unearthing and piecing together evidence that, far from being locally-contained separatist groups, many terrorist organizations in the region in fact have close and long running connections not only with each other, but to Osama bin Laden's al-Qaida as well".[29] The difference between terrorism pre-September 11 and as we now understand it is that the violence carried out by militant Islamic networks (as well as separatist rebel groups) is mainly expressive despite their instrumental value towards their goals. For the most part, "[political terrorism in its current form] is expressive, not instrumental, for it is not intended to change the world."[30] Violence serves as the main mode of expression and its purpose is symbolic. Such "[s]ymbolism involves the meaning and use [that] violence has for the victim (anxiety and humiliation, both of which were involved on September 11 [2001]) and for the offender (status, prestige, and reputation in his own group, in this case the Islamic world)."[31]

Unlike piracy in Southeast Asia, no substantive acts of maritime terrorism as an extension of terrorism itself have been carried out in the region to date. The increased perception of a maritime terrorist threat in Southeast Asia resulted in large part from the Bali terrorist bombing on 12 October 2002 by members of the Jemaah Islamiyah (JI) group, the regional affiliate of the al-Qaida. Terrorism expert David Claridge of Janusian Securities believes that this attack was a declaration of war on the global economy.[32] According to him, "[al-Qaida] has started to shift its strategy towards economic targets", which include commercial shipping lanes.[33]

There are three precedents for maritime terrorist acts. According to Singapore intelligence sources, the masterminds of the USS Cole actually planned another attack on a US ship visiting a Malaysian port in 2001. Early in 2002, Singapore intelligence disrupted an al-Qaida plot to attack a US ship docked in Singapore. Senior al-Qaida operative, Omar al-Faruq, who is now in American custody, also told officials of plans to attack an American naval ship in Surabaya, Indonesia's second largest port.[34]

Despite the crippling of the JI's operations and leadership through the arrest of individuals such as Abu Bakar Bashir (founder and "spiritual leader"), Riduan Isamuddin also known as "Hambali" (head of operations) and those who executed the Bali bombings, the group still poses a grave threat in the region. The JI bombings of a luxury hotel in Jakarta on 6 August 2003 is the most recent testament. In fact, this attack was carried out by Unit Khos, a special JI squad made up of suicide bombers "gearing up for more attacks".[35] A hardcore terrorist and expert bomb-maker known as Dulmatin (nicknamed "Genius") is expected to be the next in command in the JI hierarchy.[36] Al-Qaida, which also claimed responsibility for the Jakarta bombings, is now believed to be sustained by a "third generation" of 800 to 1,000 terrorists "ready to carry out self-managed, self-financed attacks" according to the latest UN Terrorism Committee Report.[37]

Intelligence analysts believe that because of the hardening of all land-based targets regional terrorist networks will instinctively target the region's maritime infrastructure, the remaining "soft belly" of states. Because port security has been significantly stepped up since the September 11 2001 attacks, the nature of maritime attacks in Southeast Asia will most likely be on steaming ships especially along the Malacca Straits where ships are most vulnerable to attacks and where devastation will be greatest.

If regional terrorist groups are able to sustain their operations, the likely trend for maritime terrorism in Southeast Asia will probably be:

(1) *suicide attacks on commercial and military vessels as well as ports* similar to the attacks on the USS Cole and the Limburg. With the increase in port security in the region, the remaining "soft" targets for terrorists will be ships steaming along passages such as the Malacca Straits;

(2) *hijacking* for the purposes of:

   (a) *Carrying out a subsequent suicide attack* on an unsuspecting ship or port (in the spirit of the September 11 attacks);

   (b) *Seeking ransom.* Terrorists may want to trade hostages for members of their group detained by regional authorities;

   (c) *Smuggling weapons and explosives* to their affiliates in other parts of the world. They may do this by hijacking a ship before renaming and repainting it, and providing a new crew and manifest before carry out such an operation; and

   (d) *As an act of piracy.* Terrorists may carry out acts of piracy for purposes of procuring alternative revenue for their main operations. The recent spate of pirate attacks by Acehnese rebels — though distinct from terrorists — along the Malacca Straits reflects how paramilitary organizations (whether nationalist or transnationalist in nature) may choose to turn towards certain forms of criminal activities in order to generate revenue.[38]

As forewarned by the dangers posed by current trends in piracy, suicide maritime attacks and hijacking for the purposes of carrying out such attacks pose serious threats to the maritime security of the region, especially along the Malacca Straits. Two-thirds of the world's liquefied natural gas (LNG) trade passes through the Straits. As Joseph J. Brandon, Associate Director of The Asia Foundation in Washington, put it bluntly:

> If terrorists were to commandeer a ship transporting LNG to undergo a suicide mission in the Straits of Malacca, such an act could devastate Southeast Asia's economies and environment and severely disrupt trade as the Straits could be closed to shipping and fishing.[39]

This sentiment was expressed by the IMB's Piracy Reporting Centre in Kuala Lumpur in early 2002. "Ships carrying huge loads of highly flammable gas could be hijacked by terrorists and used in suicide attacks".[40]

The State of the Art of Fighting Piracy and Maritime Terrorism in Southeast Asia

Fighting Piracy

It is clear that the efforts by Southeast Asian governments, international organizations, and shipping industries in dealing with the problem of piracy need to be stepped up.[41] "Although nations have agreed to discourage and punish [them], pirate acts are on the rise with every passing year and at and alarming rate."[42] There are several reasons for this.

First, more radical initiatives in dealing with piracy are absent because the problem is not given the kind of attention it deserves. "[People] round the world simply do not recognize that piracy really exists as a modern menace" in contrast to other threats such as international terrorism, the proliferation of weapons of mass destruction and epidemiological threats such as AIDS.[43] In Southeast Asia, except for terrorism, most non-traditional security issues are supplanted by traditional security concerns despite a broadening of the security agenda in the region.[44]

Second, there continues to exist a "lack of agreed definitions" of what constitutes piracy, which is one of "the major difficulties faced by government authorities and organizations in dealing with the problem of piracy".[45] Third, the close geographical proximity of most Southeast Asian states to waters where piracy is rampant creates a situation where current provisions within international law concerning piracy do not apply. As it is now well known, the term "armed robbery at sea" has to be applied in place of "piracy" because they do not take place on the high seas or in the exclusive economic zone. "Therefore, the law of piracy in the 1982 [UNC)LOS Convention appears to be a weak tool for preventing and suppressing attacks on ships in Southeast Asia."[46]

This is especially so along the Malacca Straits which fall under the territorial sea limits of Indonesia, Malaysia, and Singapore. Although it is deemed an "international strait", criminal and enforcement jurisdiction resides under the territorial sovereignty of these states.[47] With respect to piracy, the provision of severe penalties through domestic law continues to be lacking.

Fourth, the littoral states of Indonesia, Malaysia, and Singapore continue to "jealously guard their sovereignty over territorial waters" and deny cross-boundary "hot pursuit" (or fail to operationalize it due to their inexperience with complicated nature of this doctrine) despite having created such bilateral arrangements.[48] Ultimately, it is the nature of regional institutionalism via ASEAN and the nature of bilateral relations between the states of Southeast Asia which have come in the way of effective policy implementation.

While the current initiatives by regional governments or through ASEAN in dealing with piracy, while laudable in themselves, "so far have not got past the talking stage".[49] The ASEAN approach to security co-operation-characterized by "piecemeal negotiation, a concern with sovereignty, and complicated historical and political considerations" which translates into "reactive" and "minimalist intergovernmental intervention as and when necessary" continue to stymie a more integrated and comprehensive region-wide interstate co-ordination with regards to transnational crime such as piracy.[50] "Despite greater government concern about piracy in Southeast Asia, effective regional measures to combat piracy have not been materialized".[51] Related to these issues at the bureaucratic level are inter-state and inter-agency co-ordination. "Inertia, complacency and the complexities of national pride and rivalry are ever-present elements limiting effective action to end piracy".[52] Corruption within the enforcement and regulatory agencies of some of these states exacerbates the situation.

It is the complications over territory and sovereignty which explains why the firm call by the UN and legal scholars for states to become parties to the 1988 Suppression of Unlawful Acts against the Safety of Maritime Navigation (SUA) — the most progressive convention against ship attacks — has yet to be heeded by those in Southeast Asia. As a legal avenue for states to "prosecute acts of armed robbery against ships or any other unlawful act not covered by the definition of piracy in the Convention on the Law of the Sea", the 1988 SUA Convention could be the most vital tool for combating piracy and other crimes at sea in Southeast Asia.[53] This is because "the convention would apply to such attacks whether they were committed in port, in the territorial sea, or in maritime zones outside the jurisdiction of the coastal state".[54]

Fifth, even if states in the region were to iron out the difficulties in co-ordination, some states' lack of available resources, such as a trained maritime police as well as inadequate boats and equipment, continue to negate any headway made in the intelligence gathering efforts of state agencies prior to the prevention and suppression of such attacks.[55]

Ultimately, patrolling against piracy is essentially a police function and the provision of complete security is heavily resource-dependent. The number of patrolling vessels and aircraft assigned has a direct effect on the suppression of nautical crime, "just like the number of cops in a beat city".[56] Thachuk and Tangredi observe that the "[t]he U.S. Navy has been reluctant to take the lead in counterpiracy, since that mission is seen as siphoning resources away from primary missions of deterring war and conducting combat operations".[57] The same can be said among the navies of the littoral states in Southeast Asia since the security of the region is still highly fluid in terms of a competitive rather than "mutually reciprocated-based behaviour".[58]

In the end, the last lines of defence against piracy, and maritime terrorism are left undertaken by nongovernmental organizations such as the IMB and the International Labour Organization (ILO). First, the IMB Piracy Reporting Centre in Kuala Lumpur, established since 1992, issues regular reports of piracy via routine radio communication broadcasts and the Internet. Second, the use an anti-boarding system called Secure-Ship involving a 9,000-volt, non-lethal, electric fence surrounding a ship to prevent unauthorized boarding was recommended by the IMB made in late 2002. Third, in June 2003, the ILO implemented the issuing of a new internationally recognized identity card to the world's 1.2 million seafarers containing their photographs and biometric data which identifies fingerprints in order to prevent the disguised boarding of pirate and terrorist crews.[59]

Fighting Maritime Terrorism

The current fight against maritime terrorism in Southeast Asia is part of the fight against terrorism in general. Thus, the state of the art of anti-maritime terrorism efforts must be discussed in large part within the context of the broader campaign against terrorism.

At the international level, the decision of the IMO's Legal Committee — following the unanimous adoption in November 2001 by the IMO Assembly of resolution A.924(22) calling for a review of measures and procedures to prevent acts of terrorism which threaten the security of passengers and crews and the safety of ships — to review the SUA Convention during its 86th session in April 2003 marks a significant step towards establishing the legal provisions in dealing with maritime terrorism as a serious threat. "The proposed amendments would significantly broaden the range of offences and make it more relevant to modern conditions."[60]

At the regional level, despite the rise of international terrorism through the activities of al-Qaida and the vicious attacks carried out by radical Islamic groups, including by the 11 that have been identified in the region, the effort to counter this threat unilaterally and collectively has been mixed at best. While countries such as Singapore and Malaysia have displayed firmness in dealing with the terrorist threat by hunting down key terrorist figures and cell groups, Indonesia and Thailand were in a "denial mode" and dismissed external warnings until recently.[61] In the case of Indonesia, current criticism includes the existence of an "irresolute government response...attributed to weak political leadership, weak security apparatus" and the "absence of anti-terrorist legislation".[62]

On a brighter note, the arrest and trial of the key masterminds of the Bali bombings and the stepping up of its security laws following the Jakarta bombings has shown that the Indonesian government can muster the political will against terrorism if it wants to.[63] Also, almost all the states in the region have heightened the security and protection of potential "land-based targets" such as embassies, commercial buildings, key installations and ports. However, as already noted, the security and protection of vital sea-lanes such as the Malacca Straits and of ships passing through them have not been achieved. This prognosis has been validated by acts of piracy in these waters. Further, the same obstacles that impede regional co-operation against piracy also hamper efforts against acts of maritime terrorism.

The 11 September attacks in 2001 and the Bali bombings have also compelled ASEAN member states to establish weightier official declarations and agreements to tackle terrorism.[64] Further declarations and agreements have been made separately between ASEAN and the United States, China, and the European Union since 2002.[65] The ASEAN approach in combating terrorism was reflected in the ASEAN Summit in Bandar Seri Begawan in November 2001. While recognizing the need for member states to counter, prevent, and suppress all terrorist acts in accordance with the UN Charter, it qualified its commitment on the basis of the framework already established in fighting transnational crime. It also cautioned the need to take into account the "specific circumstances in the region and each member country" in considering joint action.[66] Such complications were involved in the trilateral anti-terrorism agreement signed by Malaysia, Indonesia, and the Philippines in May 2002 when it was extended to other ASEAN members:

> Its very broad coverage beyond targeting potential terrorist threats and the politically and legally contentious aspects of the other areas covered — such as, information-sharing on money laundering, piracy, hijacking, intrusions, illegal entry, drug trafficking, theft of marine resources, marine

pollution and illicit arms trade — created reticence on the part of other ASEAN members.[67]

These complications add to the current challenge of defining terrorism, which ASEAN, like the UN and other international bodies, has yet to overcome. After the ASEAN Home Affairs and Interior Ministers failed to define terrorism in May 2002, the caveat that "the sovereignty, territorial integrity and domestic laws of each ASEAN Member Country" be respected in the fight against this threat was reiterated.[68]

In the final analysis, despite the increasing acknowledgement that maritime terrorism poses a real threat to shipping in the region, there are no substantive contingencies and arrangements between the littoral states of Southeast Asia to deal with an emergency situation in which maritime terrorists have hijacked a ship with the intention of steering it towards another ship or a port facility. No procedures involving the use of special military or police forces in apprehending a hijacked ship or in dealing with post-attack contingencies are known to have been established.[69]

Fighting Piracy and Maritime Terrorism as "Transnational Crimes"

Despite the problems cited above, the serious attention given to terrorism by states in Southeast Asia has helped to move the regional security agenda forward. International terrorism has sharpened attention on a broad spectrum of related transnational, non-conventional security threats including piracy as outlined in the May 2002 trilateral agreement between Malaysia, Indonesia, and the Philippines against terrorism. In fact, this has injected greater brevity into previous and subsequent agreements on countering transnational crime.

While ASEAN is careful not to stretch the linkages between phenomena such as piracy, terrorism, arms smuggling, money-laundering, and other crimes, it embraces the need for more integrated approaches in dealing with them. For example, in Paragraph 4 of the Joint Declaration of ASEAN and China on Co-operation in the Field of Non-Traditional Security Issues signed at the 6th ASEAN-China Summit in Phnom Penh on 4 November 2002, member states

> [recognize] the complexity and deep-rooted background of the[se] non-traditional security issues and the need to address them with an integrated approach that combines political, economic, diplomatic, legal, scientific and technological and other means.[70]

In all likelihood, the suggestion of "holism" fits well into the modality of minimalist intergovernmental co-ordination typifying ASEAN, which has traditionally espoused the principle of non-interference in the domestic affairs of its members.

Piracy and Maritime Terrorism: Couple or Decouple?

The debate concerning the similarities or conflation between piracy and maritime terrorism in Southeast Asia has moved to the foreground recently in light of the developments of both phenomena in the region as well as their commonality as crimes of a transnational nature. Indeed, an increasing number of analysts and scholars point out that piracy and maritime terrorism have come to inhabit a common ground in four main interconnecting areas.

First, both piracy and "acts of terrorism", on the basis of international law, are transnational threats to the security of the global community.[71] In other words, "like terrorism, piracy at sea is an international [or transnational] crime."[72] Second, the tactics and approaches used in both activities do overlap.[73] Third, both employ a similar arsenal, and hence violence, in achieving their objectives. Here, hijacking may become the commonality between piracy and maritime terrorism. Fourth, there has arisen the contentious argument that because "the trend in modern piracy is becoming more bloody and ruthless" (meaning that it has become more violent) it "is also a form of terrorism that affects the crew, passengers and ship owners".[74] This overlap is further illustrated and described in Figure 3.1.

In Southeast Asia, the overlap between extreme acts of piracy and maritime terrorism — in substantive terms as well as in terms of how such threats are socially perceived — is *greatest* because of the level of violence involved in their *modus operandi* and the devastating *impact* these acts can and do have upon the safety of people and international maritime navigation.

The remaining barrier between extreme acts of piracy and maritime terrorism is a legal and definitional one and is usually described in the following manner:

> Terrorism is distinct from piracy in a straightforward manner. Piracy is a crime motivated by greed, and thus predicated on financial gain. [Maritime t]errorism is motivated by political goals beyond the immediate act of

FIGURE 3.1
The Overlap Between Piracy and Maritime Terrorism

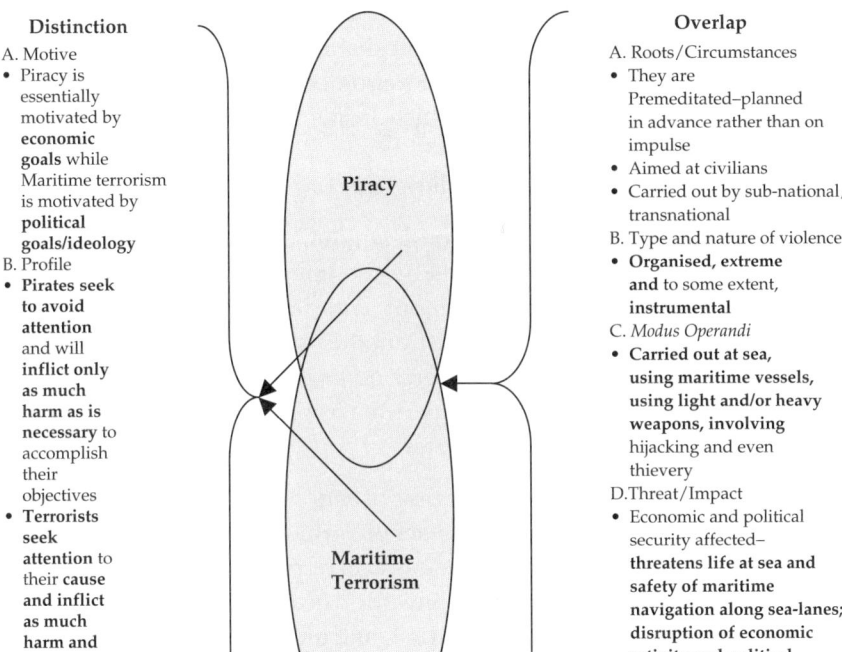

Distinction

A. Motive
- Piracy is essentially motivated by **economic goals** while Maritime terrorism is motivated by **political goals/ideology**
B. Profile
- **Pirates seek to avoid attention and will inflict only as much harm as is necessary to** accomplish their objectives
- **Terrorists seek attention to their cause and inflict as much harm and damage as possible**
C. Not all piracy involves acts of Violence

Piracy

Maritime Terrorism

Overlap

A. Roots/Circumstances
- They are Premeditated–planned in advance rather than on impulse
- Aimed at civilians
- Carried out by sub-national/ transnational
B. Type and nature of violence
- **Organised, extreme and to some extent, instrumental**
C. *Modus Operandi*
- **Carried out at sea, using maritime vessels, using light and/or heavy weapons, involving** hijacking and even thievery
D. Threat/Impact
- Economic and political security affected– **threatens life at sea and safety of maritime navigation along sea-lanes; disruption of economic activity and political stability; social climate of fear/terror**
E. Elements of legal definitions overlap

attacking or hijacking a maritime target. The motivating factor for terrorists is generally political ideology stemming from perceived injustices, both historical and contemporary.[75]

Proponents of this perspective add another distinction: "pirates want to avoid attention and will inflict only as much harm and damage as is necessary to accomplish their mission" while "terrorists…want to call attention to their cause and inflict as much harm and damage as possible."[76] That is, pirates want to sustain their trade; an act of maritime terrorism is often pyrrhic.

These distinctions are highly valid. However, they are based to a large degree upon extraneous assumptions. Crucially, with some exception given to the role of "political ideology" and "financial gain" (economics), there is nothing in the letter of the law that distinguishes an act of maritime terrorism from piracy except for the notion of "private ends". In Article 101 of UNCLOS (cited in part), which forms the basis for the working definition used by the IMO:

Piracy consists of any of the follow acts:

(a) any illegal acts of violence or detention, or any act of depredation, committed for private ends by the crew or the passengers of a private ship or a private aircraft, and directed:
  (i) on the high seas, against another ship or aircraft, or against persons or private property on board such ship or aircraft;
  (ii) against a ship, aircraft, persons or property in a place outside the jurisdiction of any State;[77]

In fact, the Article focuses on the course of action involved and not strictly on motive. The same applies to the act of "armed robbery against ships" which the IMO legally distinguishes as acts of piracy carried out "within a State's jurisdiction" which may include "ocean areas within a state's jurisdiction, such as ports, territorial sea, and archipelagic waters" or even "attacks on ships in internal waters such as lakes and rivers".[78]

Ultimately, the issue of "private ends" is a matter of arguable interpretation despite the staunch defence for its exclusivity with regards to piracy.[79] It can be easily argued that terrorism in large part is an act carried out for private ends by a group of individuals; their political ideology is not shared by the majority of the public domain. This rationale finds similar ground with the criticism raised by Czechoslovakia which objected to the insertion of the "private ends clause" during the drafting of the precursor to the 1982 LOS Convention, the 1958 Geneva Convention of the High Seas.[80]

The Czech government affirmed that the International Law Commission committed a grave omission since it did not mention acts of piracy for political ends or what some scholars classify as "politically motivated piracy" or "political piracy" which includes the attacks and seizures that are labelled as "maritime terrorism".[81] Instead, the clause was maintained and has come to find itself within Article 101 of the 1982 LOS Convention. This "shows that States have not been willing to enlarge the scope of the provisions on piracy."[82] The 1975 seizure of the Japanese flagged Sheira Maru and the 1985 hijacking of the Achille Lauro, which some interpreted as political piracy, also failed to serve as compelling cases towards pushing for accommodations within international law.[83]

However, the definition of piracy by the IMB, which crystallized at the turn of the Twenty-First Century, goes against the grain of Article 101 of the 1982 UN document. For the IMB, piracy is "an act of boarding any vessel with the intent to commit theft or any other crime and with the intent or capability to use force in the furtherance of that act."[84] Thus, "[t]he IMB definition does not require that the act of piracy be committed for private ends. Attacks on a ship for political or environmental reasons qualify as piracy." In addition, the IMB definition also abolishes the traditional two-ship requirement, "which means that attacks from a raft or even the quay are acts of piracy."[85] The IMB is obviously making an attempt at answering the call for "a more inclusive definition of piracy" in light of the "high level of maritime attacks within national territorial waters" such as those to be found in pirate prone areas of Southeast Asia.[86]

Like piracy, maritime terrorism has no internationally accepted definition to date.[87] This is partly because the definition of terrorism itself is under huge dispute.[88] Prior to the attacks upon the USS Cole and the Limburg, "the only feasible definition of maritime terrorism [was] one based on the principles of conventions dealing with aerial hijacking" which became validated through *inter alia* the bombings of hijacked airplanes such as Pan Am flight 103 over Lockerbie, Scotland in 1988 as well the 1985 bombing of an Air India jet.[89] It could be said that the maritime equivalents to Lockerbie, pre-USS Cole were the 1975 seizure of the Japanese flagged Sheira Maru and the 1985 hijacking of the Achille Lauro but without the bombings.

However, the suicidal attacks upon the USS Cole and the Limburg have obliged scholars and practitioners to look beyond these conventions. Over the last decade, some legal scholars have chosen to employ Articles 3 and 4 of the 1988 SUA Convention in order to draw up an operational definition of maritime terrorism:

(a) as any attempt of or threat to seize control of a ship by force;

(b) to damage or destroy a ship or its cargo;

(c) to injure or kill a person on board a ship;

(d) or to endanger in any way the safe navigation of a ship that moves
    from the territorial waters of one State into those of another State
    or into international waters.[90]

This application is made despite the fact that the word "terrorist" is not
mentioned in the SUA Convention as discussed earlier.

While there is no official definition of maritime terrorism among the
states of Southeast Asia either between them or through ASEAN, the
mindset of the SUA Convention is roughly applied to the definition of
maritime terrorism by the ASEAN Regional Forum's (ARF), Maritime Co-
operation Working Group of the Council for Security and Co-operation in
the Asia-Pacific (CSCAP), which is the "Track Two" or non-official level of
discussing Asia-Pacific wide security matters among ARF members.
Though it has chosen to use the US State Department's definition of
terrorism as the underlying assumption for what constitutes the
phenomenon in general — terrorism is "premeditated, politically motivated
violence perpetrated against non-combatant targets by subnational groups
or clandestine agents, usually intended to influence an audience" — the
CSCAP definition of maritime terrorism itself focuses "broadly" on
"terrorist acts and activities" in three regards:

(a) Within the marine environment;
(b) Used against vessels or fixed platforms at sea or in port, or against
    any one of their passengers or personnel;
(c) Against coastal facilities or settlements, including tourist resorts.[91]

It is no coincidence that the main elements involved in the working
definitions of maritime terrorism used in the 1988 SUA Convention as
well as the CSCAP approach are also to be found within the definitions
used in the IMB and even the IMO definition's of piracy, even despite the
latter's staunch exclusion of "political piracy" or even its defence of the
"private ends clause". In fact, the current treatment of maritime terrorism
appears to heed the call towards "defin[ing] terrorism...*in terms of what
goes on* rather than the motives for undertaking it".[92]

The "what goes on" that is most vitally shared by extreme acts of
piracy and maritime terrorism is the violence involved in both activities
and the immediate impact in terms of the threat they pose to the safety of
maritime navigation and to people and society in psychological, economic
and political terms. The "coupling" of extreme acts of piracy and maritime

terrorism is typified by the US-based Council of Foreign Relations' following observation: "Even though most people can recognize terrorism when they see it, experts have had difficulty coming up with an ironclad definition."[93] In fact, most analysts and policymakers, tend to believe that an objective and internationally accepted definition can never be agreed upon. The question of who is a terrorist, according to this school of thought, depends entirely on the subjective outlook of the definer; and, in any case, such a definition is unnecessary for the international fight against terrorism. In their view, it is sufficient to say that what looks like a terrorist, sounds like a terrorist, and behaves like a terrorist is a terrorist.[94]

By extension, acts of maritime terrorism continue to be subject to general rules and those provided by multilateral conventions for co-operation on criminal matters. Thus,

> if the co-operation of the international community on the prevention and suppression of acts of piracy is based essentially on the fact that such acts threaten the safety of maritime navigation, this argument could be made with respect to acts of maritime terrorism, maintaining *ratio reprimendi* that rules pertaining to piracy also pertain to maritime terrorism.[95]

In Southeast Asia, the case is beginning to be made in the reverse where the current threat of terrorism has sharpened the attention on other international crimes such as piracy which, while causing only as much harm and damage as is necessary to accomplish their mission can (in extreme cases) be harmful enough to inflict damage approximate to an act of maritime terrorism.

Coupling Piracy and Maritime Terrorism in Southeast Asia's Maritime Security Framework: An Agenda for Policy and Research

It is true that "long-term solutions aimed at completely eliminating piracy and terrorism may have to be fitted to the particular problem".[96] Still, the immediacy of these threats demands a decisive and an integrated set of approaches "that combines political, economic, diplomatic, legal, scientific, technological and other means" as a stop gap measure.

The current limitations by states in tackling the broad spectrum of piracy are in part due to the limitations in international law, the handicap of regional politics, and the deficiencies within current enforcement measures in Southeast Asia. Therefore, the coupling of piracy with the general threat of terrorism and, specifically, maritime terrorism as a means of both sharpening the fight against the former and in bringing greater attention to the latter (through the vulnerability of the regional maritime security exposed by piracy) should be seriously considered. Ultimately, these recommendations will fail to be implemented if the region of Southeast Asia cannot overcome the host of political obstacles that prevent them from implementing agreements and provisions at the bilateral level as well as through the ASEAN platform. Scholars and analysts have already proposed a host of workable suggestions towards effectively combating the main barrier to implementation: lack of political will.[97]

First, at the state level, countries such as Indonesia — whose archipelagic waters are rampant with piracy and whose security is most threatened by burgeoning terrorism by groups such the JI — have not been doing enough to combat these threats. Just like its previous efforts in 1992, the Indonesian coast guard and navy must continue to infiltrate archipelagic areas where pirates are believed to operate and seek shelter.[98] The Indonesian authorities, as with all other Southeast Asian states, must also intensify their efforts to pre-empt and foil terrorist attacks in the country through timely interception of suspects while they are in the planning stage of their activities.

Second, considering that the complications of the legal aspect of linking counter-piracy to the overall counter-terrorism effort have been overstated, extreme acts of piracy should be re-classified as acts akin to maritime terrorism under international law such as the 1988 SUA Convention and in regional bilateral agreements covering piracy or terrorism.[99] This would explicitly ratchet up the threat of an age-old criminal activity into a core security issue, which includes terrorism. At a minimum, by handling extreme acts of piracy under the rubric of maritime terrorism, the Indonesian government may be in a better position to deal with an embarrassing problem involving its locals who make up the majority of pirates in the region.[100]

Third, if piracy and terrorism are fused into a general threat, countries in Southeast Asia may find external assistance more palatable. "So it may be in the interest of maritime powers to "conflate" piracy and terrorism to help reluctant developing countries to let maritime powers pursue pirates and terrorists in their territorial and archipelagic waters."[101] Certainly, states such as India, Japan, and China have been showing increasing interest in conducting joint or independent naval patrols in the waters of the South China Sea. However, an increased military presence may also spur maritime terrorists to wage asymmetrical warfare against such intervening powers.

Fourth, and in relation to the second point, all Southeast Asian states must be pressured (as they currently are by the United States) into becoming parties to the 1988 SUA Convention. Asian middle powers such China and Japan have already signed the convention, as an extension of their interests in having their naval patrols "licensed" by international law.

The convention will solve other regional problems in fighting piracy and maritime terrorism. For example, the convention makes clear that the motive of the person committing the offence is not relevant. "If the person seizes control over the ship by force, the person has committed an offence."[102] Also, it will compel states in the region to create an extradition treaty specific to serious crimes at sea.[103] Also, signing the 1988 SUA and/or formalizing the non-traditional security roles of the ARF beyond dialogue towards operational co-ordination *vis-à-vis* member states' blue water navies and airforces would help create the formal link between the states of Southeast Asia and other extra-regional governments that have considerable experience co-ordinating and integrating responses to phenomena such as piracy and maritime terrorism, most notably the United States and governments of the European Union (EU).[104]

However, this co-operative arrangement involving external maritime powers can only come about if greater headway in the Malacca Straits can be re-defined and accepted as an "international strait" in more substantive terms. This would require allowance for the passage of international maritime navigation through waters that fall under the sovereignties of its littoral states, and provision for the more extensive exercise of regionally co-ordinated patrols (with the help of external maritime powers) on the warrant of achieving better maritime security against extreme cases of piracy and maritime terrorist attacks. The challenge is to create an arrangement which will (1) allay the "suspicion in Southeast Asia regarding the…goals of the Indian and US naval presence in the Strait of Malacca"; and (2) persuade littoral states that their "core" sovereignties will not be compromised in this endeavour.[105] At the same time, governments have to be reminded that they are indirectly responsible for acts of piracy and

maritime terrorism within their waters. As such, they have a vested interest
in forming co-operative arrangements with powers that have the maritime
capabilities to help secure sea-lanes along the Malacca Straits.

Conclusion

In light of the current threat of international terrorism, culminating in
the 11 September 2001 attacks, "flying planes can be dangerous".[106] This
phrase is a classic example of what linguists refer to as structurally
ambiguous since it can mean one of two things: "It can be dangerous to
pilot a plane" or "Planes in the air can be dangerous". However, with the
rise of extreme acts of piracy and (possibly) maritime terrorism, flying
planes are not the only dangerous objects we encounter today. "Ships
can be dangerous too". The structural ambiguity of this sentence conveys
the essence of the problem in which the threat of piracy and maritime
terrorism overlap each other especially in Southeast Asia. It is dangerous
for pirates or terrorists to hijack and pilot a ship in terms of the fate of the
crew and safety of maritime navigation. Ships along congested sea-lanes
such as the Malacca Straits are also dangerous since their vast presence
makes them the main medium for a "maritime spectacular" in the form
a devastating collision leading to loss of numerous lives and the crippling
the Straits.

There is a substantive basis for the coupling of extreme acts of piracy
and maritime terrorism in terms of the violence and impact they have on
people, societies, and states. This new threat modality, in addition to
helping to empower the problem-solving agenda against piracy and
terrorism, can also compel regional efforts through ASEAN and other
bilateral arrangements to be taken more seriously, particularly within a
climate of fear wrought by the rise of terrorism in general.

The management of maritime security in the region in conceptual,
legal, and operational terms requires an approach that deals with such
threats simultaneously and in an integrated fashion. The resources available
to deal with piracy and maritime terrorism are already limited. The greater
political will necessary to implement many existing solutions effectively is
also a commodity much in demand among the states in Southeast Asia.
However, until an actual incident of maritime terrorism occurs along the
Malacca Straits — one which actually causes destruction on a scale of the

2002 Bali bombing — or an extreme act of piracy which has a similar impact, it is unlikely that states in the region will be compelled to deal with these threats in a way that could have prevented them from occurring in the first place.

Notes

[1] This chapter was first prepared as a paper for Piracy Panel 1 on 5 September 2003 of the People and the Sea II Conference organized by the Centre for Maritime Research (MARE) and the International Institute for Asian Studies (IIAS) from 4 to 6 September 2003, in Amsterdam, The Netherlands. The author would like to thank the IIAS for providing the author with a grant enabling him to attend the event. The author would also like to thank the following people for their comments on the draft of this paper: Professor Robert C. Beckman, Vice-Dean (Academic Affairs) and Deputy Director, Asia-Pacific Centre for Environmental Law (APCEL) at the Faculty of Law, the National University of Singapore; and Miss Carolina Hepp, an M.A. graduate in International Peace and Security from the School of Law and Department of War Studies, King's College, University of London. The views and opinions expressed in this paper are the author's own and do not reflect those of ISEAS. Any errors are the author's own.

[2] See Robert C. Beckman, Carl Grundy-Warr, and Vivian L. Forbes, "Acts of Piracy in the Malacca and Singapore Straits", *Maritime Briefing* 1, no. 4 (United Kingdom: University of Durham, Department of Geography, International Boundaries Research Unit, 1994) p. 7; Theodore Olson, *Maritime Strategy and the New Law of the Sea: Losers and Gainers; With a Focus on Southeast Asia.* York University Centre for International and Security Studies Working Paper No. 17, August 1996, p. 13.

[3] Vijay Sakhuja, "Challenging Terrorism at Sea", Article No. 679, 19 January 2002 (Institute of Peace and Conflict Studies), <http://www.ipcs.org/issues/ newsarticles/679-ter-sakhuja.html>.

[4] Adam J. Young and Mark J. Valencia, "Piracy and terrorism threats overlap", *The Washington Times*, 7 July 2003 (The Washington Times online), <http:// dynamic.washtimes.com/print_story.cfm?StoryID=20030706-104801-9949r>.

[5] "Three S'pore ideas for boosting maritime security", *Straits Times*, 2 June 2003 (Straits Times Interactive), <http://www.straitstimes.com.sg/ storyprintfriendly/0,1887,192467,00.html>; "Remarks by Dr Tony Tan Keng Yam, Deputy Prime Minister and Minister for Defence at the Plenary session on "Maritime Security after September 11", The Second IISS Asia Security

Conference Singapore, 30 May–1 June 2003 (IISS online), <http://www.iiss.org/shangri-la-more.php?itemID=16>.

6 "Pirates should be regarded as terrorists: Kan Seng", *Business Times: Shipping Times*, 22 December 2003, p. 1.

7 Ibid., p. 1.

8 Robert C. Beckman, "Combatting Piracy and Armed Robbery Against Ships in Southeast Asia: The Way Forward", *Ocean Development & International Law*, vol. 33, p. 317.

9 *Piracy and Armed Robbery Against Ships: Report for the Period 1 January–30 June 2003* (United Kingdom: ICC International Maritime Bureau, 2003).

10 "Pirate attacks against ships increase, ICC report finds", *C.S.S. Archives* (ICC International Maritime Bureau online), <http://www.iccwbo.org/ccs/news_archives/2002/stories/piracy%20report%20Oct2002.asp>.

11 Beckman, "Combatting Piracy and Armed Robbery Against Ships in Southeast Asia", pp. 317–18.

12 "Strait of Malacca no longer a pirate haunt", *Reuters*, 9 July 2003 (Yahoo News: Singapore News), <http://sg.yahoo.com/030709/3/3cepw.html>.

13 Ibid.

14 *Piracy and Armed Robbery Against Ships: Report for the Period 1 January–30 June 2003*, p. 14.

15 Peter Chalk, *Grey-area Phenomena in Southeast Asia: Piracy, Drug Trafficking and Political Terrorism* (Canberra: Strategic and Defence Studies Centre, Research School of Pacific and Asian Studies, The Australian National University, 1997), p. 26, 32; Beckman, "Combatting Piracy and Armed Robbery Against Ships in Southeast Asia", p. 317; Joseph J. Brandon, "Piracy as Terrorism", *Journal of Commerce*, 3 June 2003, (USCIB), <http://www.uscib.org/\index.asp?documentID=2153>.

16 "Piracy soars as violence against seafarers intensifies," *C.C.S. Archives* (IMB online), <http://www.iccwbo.org/ccs/news_archives/2003/piracy_report_second_quarter.asp>; Robert C. Beckman, "Combatting Piracy and Armed Robbery Against Ships in Southeast Asia: The Way Forward", *Ocean Development & International Law*, vol. 33, p. 317.

17 Chalk, *Grey-area Phenomena in Southeast Asia*, p. 33.

18 The worldwide employment of firearms by pirates steadily increased from 0.8 per cent in 2000, to 1.4 per cent in 2001 and 2.7 per cent in 2002. See "Table 6: Comparison of types of attacks, January to June, 1992–2003", in Piracy *and Armed Robbery Against Ships: Report for the Period 1 January–30 June 2003*, p. 9.

19 See "Table 10: types of arms used by geographical locations, January to June 2003", in ibid., p. 10.

20 Indonesia alone ranked first for incidents of piracy involving hostage taking (69 out of 193) and crew members being threatened with violence (23 out of

34). It ranked second for incidents involving physical assaults (5 out of 30) and injury of crew members (6 out of 52); and third for deaths inflicted (out of 16). See "Table 8: Type of violence to crew by location, January to June 2003", in ibid., p. 9.

[21] For purposes of comparison of the data for January to June 2003, on an international scale, the incidents of piracy involving hijackings rose from 1.2 per cent (2 out 161) in January to June 2000 to 3.0 per cent (5 out of 165) in January to June 2001. The figure was 8.1 per cent for the same period in 2002 (14 out of 171) and 3.8 per cent for January to June 2003. See "Table 6: Comparison of the type of attacks, January to June" in *Piracy and Armed Robbery Against Ships: Report for the Period 1 January–30 June 2003*, p. 9.

[22] "Pirates attack small tankers in Malacca Straits" (C.S.S. Archives), <http://www.iccwbo.org/ccs/news_archives/2002/stories/tankers.asp> or "Pirate attacks against ships increase, ICC report finds" (C.S.S. Archives) <http://www.iccwbo.org/ccs/news_archives/2002/stories/piracy%20report%20Oct2002.asp>.

[23] Robert C. Beckman, Carl Grundy-Warr, and Vivian. L. Forbes, "Acts of Piracy in the Malacca and Singapore Straits", *Maritime Briefing* 1, no. 4 (United Kingdom: University of Durham, Department of Geography, International Boundaries Research Unit), p. 11.

[24] Brandon, "Piracy as Terrorism".

[25] Young and Valencia, "Conflation of piracy and terrorism in Southeast Asia", p. 267.

[26] Chalk, *Grey-area Phenomena in Southeast Asia*, p. 55.

[27] See Chalk, *Grey area Phenomena in Southeast Asia*, p. 73.

[28] "Al Qaeda in Southeast Asia: Evidence and Response" (Centre for Defence Information Terrorism Project), <http://www.cdi.org/terrorism/sea-pr.cfm>.

[29] Ibid.

[30] Christopher Coker, *Waging War without Warriors? The Changing Culture of Military Conflict*. IISS Studies in International Security (London: Lynne Rienner, 2002), pp. 4–5.

[31] Ibid., p. 5.

[32] Maria Ressa, "Maritime terror attack alert", CNN 23 October 2002, (CNN.com), <http://asia.cnn.com/2002/WORLD/asiapcf/southeast/10/23/singapore.sealane/>.

[33] Ibid.

[34] "Remarks by Dr Tony Tan Keng Yam, Deputy Prime Minister and Minister for Defence, at the Plenary session on "Maritime Security after September 11", The Second IISS Asia Security Conference, Singapore, 30 May–1 June 2003 (IISS online), <http://www.iiss.org/shangri-la-more.php?itemID=16>; Tanner Campbell and Rohan Gunaratna, "Maritime Terrorism, Piracy and Crime", in

Terrorism in the Asia-Pacific: Threat and Response, edited by Rohan Gunaratna (Singapore: Eastern Universities Press, 2003) p. 78; Maria Ressa, "Maritime terror attack alert", CNN 23 October 2002, (CNN.com), <http://asia.cnn.com/2002/WORLD/asiapcf/southeast/10/23/singapore.sealane/>.

35   "JI suicide squad on the loose", *Straits Times*, 13 August 2003, p. 1.

36   " 'Genius' could replace Hambali", *Streats*, 18 August 2003, p. 16.

37   "Al-Qaeda 3rd wave 'ready to strike' ", *Straits Times*, 28 June 2003, p. 1.

38   "Aceh rebels 'behind spate of pirate attacks' ", *Straits Times*, 14 August 2003 (Straits Times Interactive), <http://straitstimes.asia1.com.sg/asia/story/0,4386,204663-1060898340,00.html>.

39   Brandon, "Piracy as Terrorism". Brandon adds: "Moreover, significant impedance of the flow of oil would be a direct threat to the national security of countries that are energy-dependent, particularly Japan and South Korea."

40   "Tankers, gas carriers could be used as terror weapons, piracy watchdog warns", San Diego Union Tribune 4 February 2002 (SignOnSanDiego.com), <http://www.signonsandiego.com/news/nation/terror/20020204-0741-attacks-piracy.html>.

41   Carolin Liss, "Maritime Piracy in Southeast Asia", in *Southeast Asian Affairs 2003* (Singapore: Institute of Southeast Asian Studies, 2003), p. 65.

42   42 Jack A. Gottschalk, and Brian P. Flanagan, *Jolly Roger with an Uzi: The Rise and Threat of Modern Piracy* (Annapolis, Maryland: Naval Institute Press, 2000), p. 22.

43   Ibid., p. 22.

44   William T. Tow, "Alternative Security Models", in *Non-Traditional Security Issues in Southeast Asia*, edited by Andrew H. Tan and J.D. Kenneth Boutin (Singapore: Select Publishing for Institute of Defence and Strategic Studies, Nanyang Technological University), p. 268. Despite the historical underpinnings of piracy in Southeast Asia, the recent manifestation of the problem in significant terms only after the end of the Cold War-through the impact of globalization and technological development has turned an apparently traditional activity into a non-traditional security issue. *See* Carolin Liss, "Maritime Piracy in Southeast Asia", in *Southeast Asian Affairs 2003* (Singapore: Institute of Southeast Asian Studies, 2003), p. 57.

45   Beckman, "Combatting Piracy and Armed Robbery Against Ships in Southeast Asia", p. 319.

46   In fact, as it is now well known, the term "armed robbery at sea" has to be applied in place of "piracy" because piracy only takes place on the high seas. "Therefore, the law of piracy in the 1982 UNCLOS Convention appears to be a weak tool for preventing and suppressing attacks on ships in Southeast Asia." Beckman, "Combatting Piracy and Armed Robbery Against Ships in Southeast Asia", p. 328. Ibid., p. 318.

47 Beckman, Grundy-Warr, and Forbes, "Acts of Piracy in the Malacca and Singapore Straits", p. 6.

48 Young, and Valencia, "Piracy and terrorism threats overlap"; Beckman, "Combatting Piracy and Armed Robbery Against Ships in Southeast Asia", p. 330; Halloran, "What if Asia's pirates and terrorists joined hands?" Worst, the doctrine of hot pursuit is rejected by nations along the South China Sea.

49 Halloran, "What if Asia's pirates and terrorists joined hands?"; Jason Abbot, and Neil Renwick, "Maritime Piracy and Societal Security in Southeast Asia", *Pacifica Review: Peace, Security and Global Change* 11, no. 1, p. 19.

50 Chalk, *Grey-area Phenomena in Southeast Asia*, pp. 89–90; Brandon, "Piracy as Terrorism".

51 Ibid.

52 Jason Abbot, and Neil Renwick, "Maritime Piracy and Societal Security in Southeast Asia", *Pacifica Review: Peace, Security and Global Change* 11, no. 1, p. 19.

53 *United Nations Convention on the Law of the Sea: 20th Anniversary (1982–2002)*, p. 8. Available at (UN online), <http://www.un.org/Depts/los/convention_agreements/convention_20years/oceanssourceoflife.pdf>; Beckman, "Combatting Piracy and Armed Robbery Against Ships in Southeast Asia," p. 330.

54 Ibid., p. 330.

55 55 Jason Abbot, and Neil Renwick, "Maritime Piracy and Societal Security in Southeast Asia," *Pacifica Review: Peace, Security and Global Change* 11, no. 1, p. 19; Richard Halloran, "What if Asia's pirates and terrorists joined hands?" South China Morning Post, 17 May 2003 (USCIB), <http://www.uscib.org/index.asp?documentID=2636>. Ultimately, as Thacuk and Tangredi argue, patrolling against piracy is essentially a police function and is heavily resource-dependent in providing complete security. The number of patrolling vessels and aircraft assigned has a direct effect on the suppression of nautical crime, "just like the number of cops in a beat city". They also observe that the "[t]he U.S. Navy has been reluctant to take the lead in counterpiracy, since that mission is seen as siphoning resources away from primary missions of deterring war and conducting combat operations." The same can be said among the navies of the littoral states in Southeast Asia since the security of the region is still highly fluid in terms of a competitive rather than "mutually reciprocated-based behaviour" as Peter Chalk argues. See Kimberly L. Thachuk and Sam J. Tangredi, "Transnational Threats and Maritime Responses", in *Globalization and Maritime Power*, edited by Sam J. Tangredi (Washington D.C.: National Defense University Press), p. 70; Chalk, *Grey-area Phenomena in Southeast Asia*, p. 91.

56 *See* Kimberly L. Thachuk and Sam J. Tangredi, "Transnational Threats and

Maritime Responses", in *Globalization and Maritime Power*, edited by Sam J. Tangredi (Washington D.C.: National Defense University Press), p. 70.

[57] Ibid.

[58] Chalk, *Grey-area Phenomena in Southeast Asia*, p. 91.

[59] See *Piracy and Armed Robbery Against Ships: Annual Report 1 January–31 January 2002* (United Kingdom: ICC International Maritime Bureau, 2002) p. 2; "Radical plans to combat piracy in high seas", *Straits Times*, 24 October 2002; "1.2m seafarers worldwide to get ID cards", *Straits Times*, 18 June 2003, p. 4.

[60] "Legal Committee, 86th session: 28 April–2 May 2003" (International Maritime Organization), <http://www.imo.org/Newsroom/mainframe.asp?topic_id=280&doc_id=26 78>.

[61] Chin Kin Wah, "Southeast Asia in 2002: From Bali to Iraq — Co-operating for Security", *Southeast Asian Affairs 2003* (Singapore: Institute of Southeast Asian Studies, 2003) pp. 10–11 and 14.

[62] Chin Kin Wah, "Southeast Asia in 2002: From Bali to Iraq — Co-operating for Security", *Southeast Asian Affairs 2003* (Singapore: Institute of Southeast Asian Studies, 2003) p. 10.

[63] See "Jakarta alert for fresh terror attacks", *Straits Times*, 7 August 2003, p. 1.

[64] These include the Joint Communiqué of the Special ASEAN Ministerial Meeting on Terrorism adopted in Kuala Lumpur (Malaysia) on 21 May 2003; the 2001 ASEAN Declaration on Joint Action to Counter Terrorism adopted in Bandar Seri Begawan (Brunei Darussalam) on 5 November 2001, and the Declaration on Terrorism by the 8th ASEAN Summit adopted in Phnom Penh on 3 November 2002.

[65] These include the ASEAN-United States of America Joint Declaration for Co-operation to Combat International Terrorism signed in Bandar Seri Begawan on 1 August 2002; the Joint Declaration of ASEAN and China on Co-operation in the Field of Non-Traditional Security Issues signed at the 6th ASEAN-China Summit in Phnom Penh on 4 November 2002; and the Joint Declaration on Co-operation to Combat Terrorism signed at the 14 ASEAN-EU Ministerial Meeting in Brussels on 28 January 2003. Statements have also been made by the ARF such as the ARF Statement on Measures Against Terrorist Financing signed on 30 July 2002 in support of UN Security Council Resolution 1373. While these documents acknowledge the threat of terrorism as a serious issue and the need for deeper co-operation between governments, the military as well as their police and intelligence agencies, they have yet to materialize into action.

[66] Chin, Kin Wah, "Southeast Asia in 2002: From Bali to Iraq — Co-operating for Security", in *Southeast Asian Affairs 2003* (Singapore: Institute of Southeast Asian Studies, 2003), p. 16.

67 Ibid., p. 17.

68 "Work Programme to Implement the ASEAN Plan of Action to Combat Transnational Crime, Kuala Lumpur", 17 May 2002 (ASEAN Secretariat online), <http://www.aseansec.org/5953.htm>; Chin, Kin Wah, "Southeast Asia in 2002: From Bali to Iraq — Co-operating for Security", in *Southeast Asian Affairs 2003* (Singapore: Institute of Southeast Asian Studies, 2003), p. 16.

69 The author would like to thank Professor Beckman for this point, which arose in a private discussion on 22 August 2003.

70 "Joint Declaration of ASEAN and China on Co-operation in the Field of Non-Traditional Security Issues", 6th ASEAN-China Summit, Phnom Penh, Cambodia, 4 November 2002, (ASEAN Secretariat online), <http://www.aseansec.org/13186.htm>.

71 Kimberly L. Thachuk and Sam J. Tangredi, "Transnational Threats and Maritime Responses", in *Globalization and Maritime Power*, edited by Sam J. Tangredi (Washington D.C.: National Defense University Press), p. 70.

72 Kimberly L. Thachuk and Sam J. Tangredi, "Transnational Threats and Maritime Responses", in *Globalization and Maritime Power*, edited by Sam J. Tangredi (Washington D.C.: National Defense University Press), p. 70.

73 Brandon, "Piracy as Terrorism"; Young and Valencia, "Piracy and terrorism threats overlap"; Halloran, "What if Asia's pirates and terrorists joined hands?"

74 Brandon, "Piracy as Terrorism"; Sakhuja, "Challenging Terrorism at Sea".

75 Young and Valencia, "Piracy and terrorism threats overlap".

76 Young and Valencia, "Conflation of piracy and terrorism in Southeast Asia", p. 276.

77 The rest of the Article states that: "(b) any act of voluntary participation in the operation of a ship or an aircraft with knowledge of facts making it a pirate ship or aircraft; (c) any act of inciting or of intentionally facilitating an act described in subparagraph (a) or (b)." The IMO defines piracy as "unlawful acts as defined in article 101 of the 1982 United Nations Convention on the Law of the Sea." For example, see *Piracy and Armed Robbery Against Ships: Annual Report 1 January–31 January 2002* (United Kingdom: ICC International Maritime Bureau, 2002) p. 3.

78 "United Nations Convention on the Law of the Sea", in *Blackstone's International Law Documents*, 4th ed., edited by M. Evans (London: Blackstone Press Ltd, 1999), p. 231; Beckman, "Combatting Piracy and Armed Robbery Against Ships in Southeast Asia: The Way Forward", *Ocean Development & International Law*, vol. 33 Beckman, "Combatting Piracy and Armed Robbery Against Ships in Southeast Asia", p. 319.

79 Umberto Leanza and Luigi Sico, "Compensation for Victims of Maritime Terrorism", in *Maritime Terrorism and International Law*, edited by Natalino

Ronzitti (Dordrecht: Martinus Nijhoff Publishers, 1990), p. 104, Note 4; Jack A. Gottschalk, and Brian P. Flanagan, *Jolly Roger with an Uzi: The Rise and Threat of Modern Piracy* (Annapolis, Maryland: Naval Institute Press, 2000), p. 35.

[80] Natalino Ronzitti, "The Law of the Sea and the Use of Force Against Terrorist Activities", in *Maritime Terrorism and International Law*, edited by Natalino Ronzitti (Dordrecht: Martinus Nijhoff Publishers, 1990), p. 2.

[81] Ibid., p. 2; Beckman, Grundy-Warr, and Forbes, "Acts of Piracy in the Malacca and Singapore Straits", p. 10, Footnote 17.

[82] Ronzitti, "The Law of the Sea and the Use of Force Against Terrorist Activities", p. 2.

[83] Beckman, Grundy-Warr, and Forbes, "Acts of Piracy in the Malacca and Singapore Straits", p. 11, Footnote 17. The Sheira Maru was seized by a Filipino rebel group in protest against President Marcos' regime. A group of Palestinian guerrillas hijacked the Italian cruise ship Achille Lauro while it was in Egyptian territorial waters. The perpetrators threatened to kill the British and American passengers on board should a group of Palestinian prisoners held by the Israeli authorities not be released.

[84] *Piracy and Armed Robbery Against Ships: Report for the Period 1 January–30 June 2003* (United Kingdom: ICC International Maritime Bureau, 2003), p. 3.

[85] Derek Johnson and Erika Pladdet, "An Overview of Current Concerns in Piracy Studies and New Directions for Research". Position Paper for the Piracy Panels and Roundtable of the "People and the Sea II: Threats and Opportunities" Conference organized by the Centre for Maritime Research (MARE) and the International Institute for Asian Studies (IIAS), 4–6 September 2003, Amsterdam, The Netherlands, p. 4.

[86] *See* Jason Abbot, and Neil Renwick, "Maritime Piracy and Societal Security in Southeast Asia", *Pacifica Review: Peace, Security and Global Change* 11, no. 1, p. 11.

[87] Metaparti Satya Prakash, "Maritime Terrorism: Threats to Port and Container Security and Scope for Regional Co-operation". Paper presented at the 12th Meeting of the Council for Security and Co-operation in the Asia-Pacific (CSCAP) Working Group on Maritime Co-operation, Singapore, 10–11 December 2002, p. 1; Leanza and Sico, "Compensation for Victims of Maritime Terrorism", p. 97.

[88] Boaz Ganor, "Terrorism: No Prohibition Without Definition", 7 October 2001, (International Policy Institute for Counter-Terrorism), <http://www.ict.org.il/ articles/articledet.cfm?articleid=393>; Michael Nicholson, *International Relations: A Concise Introduction, 2nd ed.* (New York: Palgrave Macmillan, 2000), p. 218; Metaparti Satya Prakash, "Maritime Terrorism: Threats to Port and Container Security and Scope for Regional Co-operation". Paper presented at the 12th Meeting of the Council for Security and Co-operation in the Asia-

Pacific (CSCAP) Working Group on Maritime Co-operation, Singapore, 10–11 December 2002, p. 1; "Terrorism: An Introduction" (Council of Foreign Relations), <http://www.terrorismanswers.com/terrorism/introduction_print.html>; "Types of Terrorism" (Council of Foreign Relations), <http://www.terrorismanswers.com/terrorism/types_print.html>.

[89] Leanza and Sico, "Compensation for Victims of Maritime Terrorism", p. 97. These include the Convention on Offences and Certain Other Acts Committed on Board Aircraft, Tokyo, 14 September, 1963; the Convention for the Suppression of Unlawful Seizure of Aircraft, The Hague, 16 December 1970; the Convention for the Suppression of Unlawful Acts Against the Safety of Civil Aviation, Montreal, 23 September 1971. *See* Leanza and Sico, "Compensation for Victims of Maritime Terrorism", p. 103, Endnote 2.

[90] Leanza and Sico, "Compensation for Victims of Maritime Terrorism", p. 97.

[91] Metaparti Satya Prakash, "Maritime Terrorism: Threats to Port and Container Security and Scope for Regional Co-operation". Paper presented at the 12th Meeting of the Council for Security and Co-operation in the Asia-Pacific (CSCAP) Working Group on Maritime Co-operation, Singapore, 10–11 December 2002, p. 1.

[92] My italics. Nicholson, *International Relations*, p. 218.

[93] "Terrorism: An Introduction" (Council of Foreign Relations), <http://www.terrorismanswers.com/terrorism/introduction_print.html>.

[94] Boaz Ganor, "Terrorism: No Prohibition Without Definition", 7 October 2001 (International Policy Institute for Counter-Terrorism), <http://www.ict.org.il/articles/articledet.cfm?articleid=393>; Young and Valencia, "Piracy and terrorism threats overlap".

[95] Leanza and Sico, "Compensation for Victims of Maritime Terrorism", p. 104, Note 4.

[96] Leanza and Sico, "Compensation for Victims of Maritime Terrorism", p. 104, Note 4.

[97] See for example Beckman, Grundy-Warr, and Forbes, "Acts of Piracy in the Malacca and Singapore Straits", pp. 15–20; Beckman, "Combatting Piracy and Armed Robbery Against Ships in Southeast Asia", pp. 326–35.

[98] In 1992, there were several indications that counter-piracy measures were being stepped up by the Indonesian authorities. In July, Indonesian naval personnel had infiltrated communities where pirates were believed to conduct their activities and successfully arrested 30 pirates. Indonesia's Western Fleet also carried out an intensive campaign to rid the Malacca Straits and adjacent sea-lanes of the pirate menace resulting in 47 arrests of suspected pirates, mostly in June 1992. Beckman, Grundy-Warr, and Forbes, "Acts of Piracy in the Malacca and Singapore Straits", p. 17.

[99] Kimberly L. Thachuk and Sam J. Tangredi, "Transnational Threats and Maritime

Responses", in *Globalization and Maritime Power*, edited by Sam J. Tangredi (Washington D.C.: National Defense University Press), p. 70.

[100] This point was suggested by Professor Beckman in a private discussion with the author on 22 August 2003 in Singapore.

[101] Young and Valencia, "Piracy and terrorism threats overlap".

[102] Beckman, "Combatting Piracy and Armed Robbery Against Ships in Southeast Asia", p. 330.

[103] This will side step the provision of a general extradition treaty covering the whole spectrum of crimes including war and political crimes as previously suggested by Chalk. *See* Chalk, *Grey-area Phenomena in Southeast Asia*, p. 92.

[104] Ibid., p. 92.

[105] Young and Valencia, "Conflation of piracy and terrorism in Southeast Asia", p. 278.

[106] Cynthia Weber, "Flying Planes Can Be Dangerous". *Millennium: Journal of International Studies* 31, no. 1, pp. 129–48.

4

Piracy and Terrorism in Southeast Asia: Similarities, Differences and Their Implications[1]

Mark J. Valencia

Introduction

On March 27 2003, the *New York Times* reported recent attacks on several chemical tankers in the Strait of Malacca region by assailants with automatic weapons.[2] Two of the ships — the Suhaila and the Oriental Salvia — were sprayed with AK-47 rifle fire in broad daylight on 25 February and 18 March respectively, while on March 26 the Dewi Madrim was boarded silently at night, commandeered for an hour and looted.[3] While some attributed the attacks to "terrorists", it was later discovered that the perpetrators were apparently only after equipment and other valuables. In other words, they were "pirates", albeit unusually bold and violent ones.

Since the events of 11 September 2001, the conflation of "piracy" and "terrorism" has become common in the mass media and government policy statements, both within and outside the region.[4] Indeed, the International Maritime Board (IMB) has warned of growing overlap between terrorists and pirate gangs, particularly in Indonesia.[5] But piracy and terrorism may have different causes, tactics, and objectives and thus may require different responses. This paper examines the similarities and differences between "piracy" and "terrorism" and their implications for approaches to addressing the problems.

Definitions: Similarities, Differences and Implications

The precise definition of "piracy"/"pirates" and "terrorism"/"terrorists" has been problematic for national and international policy makers alike. The standard international legal definition of piracy is that used in the 1982 United Nations Convention on the Law of the Sea (1982 UNCLOS), Article 101, which also appears in the 1958 United Nations Convention on the High Seas.[6] Here piracy is defined as "any illegal acts of violence or detention, or any act of depredation, committed for private ends by the crew or the passengers of a private ship or a private aircraft, and directed (i) on the high seas against another ship or aircraft, or against persons or property on board such ship or aircraft; (ii) against a ship, aircraft, persons or property in a place outside the jurisdiction of any state." Under the Law of the Sea, a piratical ship may be seized by any nation on the high seas.

The obvious problem with this definition when applied to Southeast Asia is that such acts usually occur in territorial or archipelagic waters, and thus are not legally considered piracy. There is therefore no international agreement regarding prevention of, and enforcement against most "maritime violence" or "sea robbery", and arrest and prosecution is dependent on the state in whose jurisdiction the crime occurs. The process is further complicated in Southeast Asia because uncertain or unresolved boundaries complicate the question of legal jurisdiction over the crime.

To address this problem, the IMB has defined piracy as "an act of boarding, or attempting to board any ship with the intent to commit theft or any other crime and with the intent or capability to use force in furtherance of that act".[7] Meanwhile, the International Maritime Organization has distinguished between "piracy" as previously defined and "armed robbery against ships" which means "any unlawful act of violence or detention or any act of depredation, or threat thereof, other than an act of "piracy", directed against a ship or persons or property on board such a ship, within a state's jurisdiction over such offences."[8]

Terrorism is also a complicated political concept and definitional consensus has thus been impossible. A working definition of maritime terrorism is that of "political piracy":[9] "... any illegal act directed against ships, their passengers, cargo or crew, or against sea ports with the intent of directly or indirectly influencing a government or group of individuals".[10] However, this definition does not address issues such as state-sponsored terrorism, and terrorism associated with criminal activity. Nor does it include the threat of violence.

Suppression of terrorism is circumscribed by jurisdictional limitations. Terrorism on the high seas is not punishable unless the vessel perpetrating the act was scheduled to navigate through the territorial waters of a party to the 1988 Convention for the Suppression of Unlawful Acts Against the Safety of Maritime Navigation, or the victim was a national of a state party.[11] Unlike piracy, which is accorded universal jurisdiction for both prescription and enforcement, jurisdiction for terrorism is restricted and defers to territorial sovereignty. Because of the range of definitions there is no universal prescription.

• Clearly there is some definitional overlap between piracy/sea robbery and "terrorism" in that they all can and often do involve violence at sea. However, piracy and sea robbery are illegal acts committed for private gain while terrorism is an illegal act committed with the intent of influencing a government or a polity, i.e., it has a political objective.[12] And piracy on the high seas is a universal crime and can be repressed by any nation while repression of terrorism on the high seas is legally confined to particular nations and circumstances.

The Nature of Piracy and Maritime Terrorism: Similarities, Differences and Their Implications

Piracy

Piracy/sea robbery (hereafter piracy) encompasses a wide spectrum of criminal behaviour ranging from in port pilferage, to hit and run attacks, to temporary seizure of the ship, to long-term seizure, and, at the "high end", to permanent theft of the ship. This spectrum corresponds to an escalating scale of risk and return. As the risk and potential return increase, so do the threat and degree of violence. Indeed, the more that is at stake the more the attackers are willing to use violence. Additionally, as the risk, return, and the potential for violence increase, so does the apparent degree of organization of the attackers.[13] A significant portion of piracy incidents worldwide occur in Southeast Asia,[14] and the violence of attacks appears to be increasing, including hijacking, hostage taking, and the use of firearms.

First, and by far the most common type of piracy, is hit and run theft where criminals sneak aboard a ship, generally at night, and steal what they can immediately lay their hands on, like cash and electronic equipment, with an average take of $5,000 to $15,000 in value.[15] These crimes tend to be opportunistic (i.e., not planned with a great deal of forethought) and generally accompanied by little or no violence, involving sneak thieves armed with knives, often boarding in port. Crewmembers are often not aware of their presence. This is a low investment crime, and has a low return, which translates into less violence. This of course does not mean that there is not an apparent willingness to use force. In one incident, assailants boarded a ship at dock and were surprised by the ships' crew who used anti-personnel aerosols. But in the scuffle, one of the attackers threw a metal object causing a severe head wound to a crewmember.[16] Nevertheless, as long as resistance is not encountered, these incidents are predominantly non-violent.

Temporary or short-term seizures of ships represent the next step up in the spectrum of risk, potential return, potential for violence, and level of organization of attacks. Seizing the ship, especially if it is already underway, requires boats, grappling hooks, and enough people with the means to control the crew. This necessitates a degree of co-ordination and organization. Some capital investment is required for boats and arms, training (or finding experienced people for boarding), co-ordinating a large group, and possibly for obtaining inside information regarding what a particular vessel is carrying. One example is the *Valiant Carrier* incident.[17] The ship was carrying fuel oil (a valuable and easily resalable commodity), and was attacked four hours out of Singapore in the Malacca Strait. Using Molotov cocktails to distract the crew (on a fuel oil ship!), twelve attackers boarded, and rounded up the crew, taking the captain and his family to open the safe. A deck officer was severely stabbed, the master electrician was wounded and the captain's seven-month old daughter was injured as well. The bridge was unmanned during the attack greatly enhancing the possibility of collision or running aground. The attackers jumped overboard and were picked up by waiting boats. These short-term seizures clearly present danger to sealanes, ports and the environment, and they raise the concern that such acts could easily be accomplished by terrorists. For this type of piracy, the threat of violence is obviously real, but should not be overstated.

Long-term seizure of boats is similar to short term seizure except for the duration and purpose of control. There is also an increase in risk, potential return, violence and level of organization. The goal is no longer to simply steal whatever can be taken in thirty minutes or so, but rather the whole cargo. Although the duration of control is significantly longer, the main goal is still the theft of goods on board the ship. This necessitates having a location to dock and unload cargo, or another ship to which to transfer it, a buyer of the cargo, and a plan to deal with hostages (crewmembers), provided they were not murdered in the initial takeover. The case of the *M.V. Marta* is an example of this type of piracy.[18] In 1990, the *Marta* set out from Bangkok for Busan (Republic of Korea) with a cargo of over US$2 million worth of tin plate. Four heavily armed assailants, with obvious prior knowledge of the shipment, boarded the ship and overpowered the crew. They sailed the ship southwards for two days. The cargo was then offloaded by barges and crews with forklifts. After sailing on for a couple of more days the captain was drugged and taken hostage by the pirates as they escaped. But the rest of the crew and the ship were released. Apparently the perpetrators were quite experienced as they bragged, "…that this was the sixth such successful attack they had undertaken in the last eighteen months."[19]

The most serious form of piracy is the fourth type — hijacking. Hijackers are intent on permanent seizure and thus something must be done with the crew. The tactics of hijackers are almost identical to those perpetrating short term and long term seizures. They involve armed assailants boarding the vessel while en route, controlling the crew, and taking over the ship. However, in permanent seizures the pirates need a contact to sell the cargo, and a location where the boat can be disposed of, or in some cases repainted, re-flagged and returned to service. The *Alondra Rainbow* incident in October 1999 was a classic case of hijacking, where a Japanese ship registered under a Panamanian flag was hijacked for its cargo of aluminium ingots. Before the hijackers could dispose of the entire cargo, the ship was apprehended by the Indian Navy.

Because the potential return of the attack is so high, the organization necessary so extensive, and the ultimate disposal of the crew necessary, hijacking is at the high end of the spectrum of risk, potential return, violence, and level of organization. And it obviously raises concerns that terrorists could undertake similar actions for political purposes.

The dangers of piracy thus include a direct threat to the lives and welfare of the citizens of a variety of flag states; a direct economic impact in terms of fraud, stolen cargoes, delayed trips, and increased insurance premiums; the undermining and weakening of political stability by encouraging official corruption; and the potential to cause a major environmental disaster.

Piracy is an economic crime committed for financial gain, and therefore the principal causes can be sought in prevailing economic conditions. The Asian economic crisis of the late 1990s had a deep impact on Southeast Asian countries, creating an incentive for those at the lower end of the economic scale to turn to illegal sources of income. This economic collapse also triggered widespread political instability, most notably in Indonesia, creating an environment where people could more easily pursue their illegal methods of income generation. Indeed, economic collapse, combined with endemic governmental corruption and loose political control, creates an environment in which piracy may be ignored or even tacitly enabled by corrupt military elements who may share in the "booty".[20] Another factor encouraging piracy in Southeast Asia is the relative security provided by the permeable, poorly controlled, and, in some areas, uncertain international maritime boundaries which allow pirates to easily cross borders to escape pursuit.

Maritime Terrorism

Terrorism is distinct from piracy in a very straightforward manner. While piracy is a crime motivated by greed and thus predicated on immediate financial gain, terrorism, and its maritime manifestation, "political piracy" or maritime terrorism, is motivated by political goals beyond the immediate act of attacking or hijacking a maritime target.

Terrorism at sea includes the threats of attacks on shipping, the threat of ships being used as weapons, and the threat of ships being used to deliver concealed weapons of mass destruction (in containers or within the ship's superstructure). All have the potential to cause systemic economic dislocation. Indeed, the effect of a major attack on a US port or on a transhipment hub such as Singapore would be felt globally.

For example, the aspect of tanker transportation most economically sensitive to terrorism is insurance. It is uncertain to what extent oil and liquefied natural gas (LNG) supplies would be adversely affected by a spike in insurance premiums, or withdrawal of coverage from areas of the Middle East or Southeast Asia should terrorism or war risk be judged unacceptably high. To assuage this possibility the US Department of Transportation has offered war risk insurance for vessels entering the region when commercial insurance cannot be obtained at reasonable terms. However, this would probably not be effective against mines.[21] Since the Bali bombing, war-risk status has applied to Indonesian ports, but not as yet to passage through the archipelago.[22]

In the previous paper, Ong identifies three key events that have put maritime terrorism on the "radar" of policy makers: the *Achille Lauro* hijacking, the attack on the US *Cole*, and the attack on the French supertanker *Limburg*. In addition to these incidents, the level of concern regarding maritime terror has been heightened since 11 September 2001 by the widely disseminated and largely accepted fact that al-Qaida possesses some 15 cargo vessels,[23] and the purported plan by al-Qaida affiliated operatives to attack US ships in Malaysia, Singapore, or Indonesian waters and ports.[24] Indeed, Jemaah Islamiyah is supposed to have planned attacks on supertankers in the Jurong, Bukom, and Changi areas in 2001.[25]

A captured al-Qaida suspect, Abd al-Rahim al Nashiri has reportedly admitted helping plan the attacks on the Cole and the Limburg, and has outlined a maritime terror "strategy". The first element is that employed against the Cole and the Limburg — suicide cadres operating Zodiacs filled with explosives. The second element would employ trawlers and medium size ships that could be blown up near warships or cruise liners. The third element would use explosive-laden small planes stolen from flying clubs. And the fourth element would involve underwater demolition teams.[26]

The *Achille Lauro* incident received international publicity, particularly since an American was killed during the attack. And it raised several important issues and concerns, including the almost complete lack of security and preventive measures which made it easy for a handful of

Palestinian Liberation Organization (PLO) operatives to seize the vessel. Apparently the PLO operatives had planned to carry out an attack on the Israeli port of Ashdod but a waiter happened upon them cleaning their weapons, thus forcing them to act prematurely. The PLO operatives seized control of the *Achille Lauro* and "toured" the eastern Mediterranean. Eventually the Egyptian authorities negotiated the release of the vessel in exchange for returning the PLO operatives to Palestine. However, because an American had been killed in the ordeal, then US President Reagan ordered two F-14 Tomcats to overtake the Egyptian plane taking the PLO operatives to Syria, and to escort it to Sicily where the Palestinians were arrested by Italian security.[27] The lack of security and the ease with which the cruise ship and its passengers were seized shocked the US government and raised concern regarding other potential soft targets, including other maritime targets.[28]

The attack on the French supertanker *Limburg* serves as a recent, and poignant, reminder of the potential of maritime terrorism. Apparently, a small boat, presumably packed with explosives, came alongside the *Limburg* off the coast of Yemen. Soon after, a large explosion rocked the ship. The ship caught fire and leaked 90,000 barrels of oil into the Gulf of Aden.[29] This attack came just a week before the anniversary of the similar attack on the *USS Cole.* Yemen is paying an enormous price for these attacks. Its container terminal throughput dropped from 43,000 TEU in September 2002 to 3,000 TEU in November 2002, insurance premiums rose to $300,000 per port call, and 3,000 people lost their jobs in Aden as a result.[30] These attacks further solidified US security concerns regarding maritime terrorism.

Overlaps

There is certainly some overlap between acts of piracy and actions of secessionist groups in the maritime arena. Actual examples include the ransom kidnappings undertaken purportedly by members of Abu Sayyaf in the southern Philippines and those by alleged members of the Free Aceh Movement, in which crew members were attacked and held for ransom in waters off Aceh.[31]

However, the reasons for a low rate of maritime terrorism as compared to piracy are:

1. most terrorists are "land-lubbers" with little maritime experience;
2. operating at sea requires special equipment and skills;
3. fixed land targets offer a greater ease of access;
4. despite 9/11, terrorists are traditionally tactically conservative and tend to opt for the course of least resistance; and
5. attacking a vessel on the high seas is less likely to attract international attention than more media-accessible land targets.

Nevertheless, the perceived threat of maritime terrorism has increased in recent years due to:

1. lax port security, poor coastal surveillance, a profusion of targets, and a trend toward "skeleton crews";
2. the opportunity for mass casualty attacks such as LNG carriers/terminals, refineries, petrochemical installations, and cruise ships; and
3. increased tactical sophistication as exemplified by the events of 9/11.

Thus piracy and terrorism do overlap in the tactics of ship seizures and hijackings, and the conditions which allow them to thrive, e.g., poverty, political instability, permeable international boundaries, and ineffective enforcement. However, the political objectives of terrorists distinctly separate their motivation from that of pirates. Indeed terrorists want to call attention to their cause and to inflict as much harm and damage as possible. Pirates want to avoid attention and will inflict only as much harm and damage as is necessary to accomplish their mission.

Implications of Similarities and Differences for Counter-Measures

Although the circumstances that allow piracy and terrorism to develop and grow are similar, the root causes are different. For pirates, the motivating factor is economics; for terrorists it is generally political and religious ideology stemming from perceived injustices, both historical and contemporary. Thus while the tactics of combating maritime terrorism and piracy may be similar, long-term solutions may require different approaches.

Current Counter-Measures

The 1988 SUA Convention

The *Achille Lauro* incident indirectly led to the IMO sponsorship of the 1988 Rome conference from which emerged support for a Convention for the Suppression of Unlawful Acts Against the Safety of Maritime Navigation Convention (SUA).[32] SUA was meant to "...fill many of the jurisdictional gaps highlighted when the acts endanger the safety of international navigation and occur on board national or foreign flag ships while underway in the territorial sea, international straits or international waters. The convention requires states to criminalize such acts under national law and to co-operate in the investigation and prosecution of their perpetrators".[33] Although the convention was developed in large part in response to the 1985 *Achille Lauro* incident and with the objective of combating terrorism,[34] it can also be an anti-piracy and anti-sea robbery measure.[35] Indeed, if a person seizes control of a ship by force, or threat thereof, or performs an act of violence likely to endanger the ship's safe navigation, the person has committed an offence under the convention, regardless of the motive.

The United States and other maritime powers have proposed amendments which would expand the offences under the SUA treaty to include transport of materials associated with weapons of mass destruction, and to facilitate boarding of suspect ships on the high seas.[36] And they have been pressing other countries to ratify it. But so far, only other maritime powers like Canada, major European countries, Australia, China, and Japan have ratified it. Indeed, in ASEAN only Brunei, the Philippines, Singapore and Vietnam are parties to the SUA Convention. The Convention requires states parties to co-operate to ensure the arrest and prosecution of offenders, including arrest, extradition or prosecution of such offenders, and to prevent preparations in their territories for the commission of such offences.

Some ASEAN states are unwilling to commit to prosecute persons caught in their waters for acts committed in another country's waters. And for countries with a recent colonial history and relatively newly won independence, as well as ineffective navies and disputed or porous maritime boundaries, the convention can be seen as underscoring their inability to fulfil their obligations, or even compromising their national sovereignty. Adding to their suspicion is an Intertanko-backed proposal to

establish a neutral flag fleet that would patrol the Malacca Strait and be
allowed to pursue pirates across national maritime borders.[37] This could
be perceived by the Strait States as "internationalizing" the Strait. Thus
some Southeast Asian States feel the SUA Convention only makes sense
for those countries with effective maritime forces and unchallenged
maritime boundaries.

It has been argued that in order to enforce the provisions of the 1982
United Nations Convention on the Law of the Sea concerning piracy, the
military vessel of one state might be allowed with the "courtesy" of the
coastal state to continue the pursuit of a pirate ship across territorial sea
boundaries. However, these arguments are not convincing enough to
restrict the doctrine of territorial sovereignty enjoyed by coastal states.
But, if "piracy" and "terrorism" are fused into a general threat to maritime
security, developing countries may find support of SUA as well as outside
"help" easier to accept and to "sell" to their domestic polity (cf. Ong, this
volume). So it may be in the interest of Singapore and the United States to
conflate piracy and terrorism to persuade reluctant developing countries
to assist in the pursuit of pirates and terrorists in their territorial and
archipelagic waters.

US Initiatives

Since September 11, 2001, the United States has viewed Muslim extremists
in Indonesia, Malaysia, the Philippines, and Thailand as potential threats
to world commerce flowing through Southeast Asian seaways. The
nightmare for the United States is that a supertanker will be hijacked and
driven into Singapore port, or sunk in the narrowest portion of the Malacca
Strait, possibly by use of weapons from afar, thus seriously disrupting or
detouring the flow of oil to East Asia, and potentially constraining US
naval mobility and flexibility as well. And the United States has little
confidence in the capacity and will of the Southeast Asian countries to
prevent such a disaster. Demonstrating that these concerns are real, in July
2002, Greenpeace activists using Zodiacs boarded and hijacked the 160,000-
ton Crude Dior oil tanker at the northern entrance of the Bosphorus Strait.
Although this incident ended peacefully, it showed that such hijacking
could be accomplished rather easily.[38]

The United States has undertaken, in co-operation with India, a
proactive attempt to control both piracy and terrorism in the Strait of

Malacca. Tankers and LNG carriers using the Strait are considered particularly vulnerable to "ramming" and boarding because they are slow moving and carry valuable and potentially dangerous cargo, and the Strait has high economic importance, high traffic volume and limited manoeuvrability (see Ong, this volume).[39] This effort used United States and Indian warships to escort commercial vessels of "high value", transiting the Strait. However, naval patrols by major powers may not be the most effective or politically acceptable way to combat either piracy or terrorism. Indeed, the conflation of the two phenomena may actually be a disadvantage to the United States.

First, these patrols have created suspicion in Southeast Asia regarding the real goals of the Indian and US naval presence in the Strait of Malacca. Indeed, this effort may well be viewed as an attempt to internationalize the Malacca Strait. Second, in the wake of the Cold War and the events of 9/11, the United States and India have developed a new political and military relationship. Indeed, it appears that the Bush administration may even desire a full-fledged alliance, which would make India the United States' foremost military ally in Asia. Apparently India agreed to the patrols in return for the resumption of arms sales to India, specifically the "Fire Finder" radar system.[40] This political context suggests that the Indian and US naval presence in the Strait is not just to combat piracy and terrorism, but is part of a broader attempt to assert a US-friendly Indian naval presence in the region. Thus for the United States, the joint patrols are the beginning of a larger military engagement with India.[41] And for India, the patrolling of the Malacca Strait is evidence and endorsement of its claim that its security interests stretch up to and include the Strait.

Although this may be seen by some as a reasonable attempt to create a security order in the region, others such as Indonesia and China could well view this development as a threat to their regional authority and influence. When one considers the current US military and political actions in the Muslim world, such actions by the United States and historically dominant India may not be universally viewed as positive, or constructive by Muslim Southeast Asia. Indeed the potential ability of these patrols to curb piracy and terrorism may not outweigh their potential to undermine security relations in the region.

Concerns over terrorism are driving closer co-operation among the police forces and intelligence agencies in Southeast Asia, but are also triggering distrust and cautious monitoring of neighbouring countries. All the while, a wary eye is being cast on US involvement in the region, with lingering fears that Washington will use terrorism as an excuse to impose its political will upon Asian nations. Countering this requires even more co-operation and a more grounded basis for a regional block — something some nations are mooting — but distrust and inherent competition continue to undermine such initiatives.

There are also practical issues regarding the effectiveness of US and Indian naval anti-piracy/terrorism patrols in the Strait region. Of significant concern is the arrest authority of foreign naval vessels in waters under another country's jurisdiction. Commercial ships may exercise their rights to transit through international straits, and accordingly naval vessels may escort those ships under the transit passage regime. But their authority is generally limited to their own flag vessels. "Enforcement is largely left to the navy, which possesses the hardware of enforcement but lacks the power of arrest. This role is also at odds with international practice in which navies typically operate on the high seas leaving patrolling of territorial waters to coast guard-type bodies".[42] Perhaps the purpose of the US/Indian naval escorts is simply to deter would be pirates and terrorists by the sheer intimidation of their presence, regardless of their legal authority, or to act as the eyes and ears of local maritime security forces.

There is also a question regarding the appropriate size of the pursuit craft. In the shallow waters where most pirates operate, high-speed patrol craft are of more practical value.[43] Pirates tend to be highly mobile groups that operate based on intimate local knowledge of the waters and can easily lose larger pursuers in the maze of islands in Southeast Asia.

The US Proliferation Security Initiative (PSI)

The PSI is an anti-maritime terrorism measure being applied in the region. The 24 June 2003 seizure of the cargo ship Baltic Sky by Greek commandos in Greek territorial waters, and the 1 July 2003 seizure by Spanish forces of a ship carrying South Korean rifles and 100mm guns,[44] are manifestations of this US-led anti-terrorist maritime initiative. Indeed, the Bush Administration is pressing a group of "like-minded" countries to agree to selective interdiction of ships bound to or from "rogue nations" carrying materials or technology used to manufacture or deliver weapons of mass destruction (WMD). Mid-level officials from the United States, Great Britain, Italy, Japan, Australia, France, Germany, Poland, Portugal, the Netherlands and Spain met in Madrid in mid-June 2003 to discuss this proposal, and again in Australia, on 9–10 July of the same year.

There are three basic international legal problems with this initiative. First, it is not illegal for nations who are not signatories to the Nuclear Non-proliferation Treaty or the Missile Control Technology Regime to ship nuclear materials or missiles to each other. And it is not illegal to trade commercially in explosives, or arms for that matter. Indeed in both the Baltic Sky and South Korean cases, the cargo owners claimed the shipments were a legitimate commercial transaction. Second, according to the 1982 UN Convention on the Law of the Sea, warships and government ships used only for non-commercial purposes have complete immunity from the jurisdiction of any other state on the high seas. This could include government vessels transporting weapons to other states on a non-commercial basis. Third, and far more important, such interdictions, agreed or otherwise, could undermine the carefully nurtured balance enshrined in the 1982 UNCLOS.

This treaty was a "grand bargain" between developing states and the maritime powers and is seen by most countries as a "package deal." A major bone of contention during the nearly two decades of acrimonious negotiations was the desire of developing coastal states to limit the "freedom" of navigation of the maritime powers. However, maritime powers led by the United States insisted on very broad freedom of navigation out of concern that their naval and air access and mobility could be severely restricted by the global EEZ "enclosure" movement. The contending groups finally agreed to establish three major zones.

1. A 12-nautical-mile (nm) territorial sea where coastal states retain some sovereignty over most activities and where only innocent passage is allowed, that is, passage which is not "prejudicial to the peace, good order or security of the coastal state."
2. A 200-nm Exclusive Economic Zone (EEZ) where coastal states retain sovereign rights over resources and related activities but maritime powers retain most of their high seas navigational "freedoms."
3. The high seas, where navigational freedoms remain unencumbered.

The Treaty came into force in November 1994 upon its 60th ratification. The United States Congress has yet to ratify it, but is considering doing so.

Nevertheless, the United States has long argued that the navigational freedoms codified by the Convention are customary international law.

But now the United States would like to interdict suspect vessels on the high seas, and even within other nations' territorial and archipelagic waters, presumably — but not certainly — with those countries agreement. Current international law allows interdiction and boarding of suspect vessels only with the permission of the country under whose flag the ship is sailing, or if the ship is stateless. Interdictions on the high seas would deviate from the traditional US staunch defence of freedom of navigation, and such "exceptions" could over time create new law and practice. Indeed if the United States can arrange for such "exceptions", so could other countries. What is more troubling to some nations is that the United States may proceed with interdictions in other countries' waters without their concurrence or even their knowledge.

The December 2002 forced boarding, inspection and seizure of the cargo vessel *So San* on the high seas by the Spanish warship Navarra at the behest of the United States was perhaps the first major "shot" in this new US maritime initiative. The US Navy took over the detention of the vessel from the Spanish. The vessel was technically stateless although the United States knew it had come from a North Korean port.[45] Such vessels are subject to boarding and inspection — but not seizure. Although the United States eventually released the vessel, the damage to international law and the convention had already been done.

In the Baltic Sky case, the vessel was carrying 750 tonnes of industrial grade explosives and detonators from Tunisia to Sudan. NATO alleged that the ship was operating in an abnormal and suspicious manner. But both Tunisia and the cargo buyer in Khartoum claimed the purchase and the transport of the explosives were part of a purely commercial transaction. Of course Greece may have considered that transporting such a dangerous cargo through its territorial waters was prejudicial to its security. But that may now be up to the courts, or perhaps the International Tribunal for the Law of the Sea to decide. And in the South Korean arms case, South Korea protested that the cargo was a legitimate commercial transaction with Senegal.

What are the options? The United States could try to get the U.N. Security Council to pass a resolution authorizing states to board and inspect any vessel or vehicle if there is reason to believe they are carrying weapons of mass destruction (WMD). But after its defeat in the Security Council regarding its invasion of Iraq, this is unlikely. Indeed, the fact that China is not part of this initiative and sits on the Security Council presents formidable obstacles.

The United States could try to get NATO's co-operation. According to the U.N. Charter, regional organizations, such as NATO, are permitted to take measures to secure their regions — which for NATO would be a large part of the Western world. Since WMD could pose a global threat, NATO could have broad authority to interdict weapons heading to "rogue" nations. But the administration could face considerable challenges winning NATO's support as an alliance because all NATO members must agree to the plan for it to receive alliance approval.

The United States could try to beef up the 1988 Convention for the Suppression of Unlawful Acts Against the Safety of Maritime Navigation (SUA). Indeed the United States has proposed to amend the convention to allow boarding of suspect ships on the high seas but some parties to the convention have opposed this.

Or the United States and its coalition could invoke article 51 of the UN charter arguing that in the wake of September 11, 2001, WMD in the hands of its avowed enemies constitute a clear and present threat to their security. However, the United States and its coalition would have to demonstrate that the interdicted cargo presented an imminent threat of attack — a rather difficult task.

Finally, the United States could continue its current efforts to build a coalition of nations willing to co-operate with it in this effort. Indeed, US counter-proliferation goals may be best served by expanding upon existing efforts, through enhanced surveillance and intelligence gathering. Without amending either national laws or innocent passage under UNCLOS, this would entail relying upon those states willing to co-operate, and waiting until suspect vessels or aircraft enter their territorial waters or airspace, before seizing or forcing them down.

The problem with any of these options is that some countries in the region are concerned about provoking North Korea and may not participate in the PSI. North Korea has repeatedly said it would view an embargo or interdictions as an act of war. Even Japan, which attended the PSI meetings, participates with some reluctance.[46] Indeed, Japan has claimed that the PSI does not specifically target North Korea. The use of Japanese warships on the high seas for such interdictions could raise sensitive issues for Japan both domestically and among its neighbours who suffered at Japan's hands during World War II.

But, China and most notably South Korea may not participate. If they do not, any embargo or interdiction "net" will have fatal holes and thus be largely symbolic at best. Nevertheless, it is possible that the threat of interdiction might curtail some shipments, particularly of the bulky factory equipment necessary for manufacturing WMD. However, combinations of planes, trains, or ships carrying WMD material from or to North Korea could link North Korea to other co-operative states, e.g. Pakistan or Iran, by passing through China's territory or airspace. Moreover, the effort is not focused only on WMD but on limiting international income to North Korea, which is primarily derived from arms and drug sales. So allowing legitimate commercial transport would undermine the objective of the policy. But interdicting legal shipments would undermine international law.

The PSI, if carried to its extreme, also further undermines the concept of the sovereignty of nations. Australian Foreign Minister Alexander Downer said recently that Australia no longer considered the sovereignty of other nations as absolute in international law as it is more important to end humanitarian suffering or security crises. The United States has already acted in Kosovo following a similar rationale.

Thus this new US maritime initiative runs the risk of introducing a "might makes right" regime for the Law of the Sea. As a result, this new initiative and resistance to it may stimulate a sorely needed, frank discussion of US intentions and their implications for the Law of the Sea, the concept of sovereignty, and world order in the twenty-first century.

Japanese Initiatives

On 12 March 2002, at Japan's initiative, maritime authorities and experts from 14 other Asian countries convened in Tokyo to discuss ways of combating piracy in the region.[47] Also in August 2002, the Japanese Coast Guard and the Royal Brunei Marine Police conducted a joint anti-piracy exercise in waters offshore Brunei.[48] On 23 October, Japan dispatched a Coast Guard patrol boat (the Yashima) for training in the South China Sea and joint training with the Indian Coast Guard. The Yashima made port calls in India and Singapore and patrolled nearby waters.[49] In March, after an anti-piracy conference of the region's coast guards in Manila, the

Japanese and Philippine Coast Guards led an anti-piracy training exercise.[50] In July, the Yashima participated in a training exercise in Malaysia and Japan is assisting Indonesia in drafting a coast guard code.[51] Although Japan continues to propose multilateral joint patrols, Southeast Asian nations have so far not accepted this proposal.

Indigenous Efforts and Self-Help

Coastal states must do more to improve security at ports and their approaches. The IMB has also recommended that the designated lanes used by tankers be declared "no-go" areas for unauthorized craft, enforced by intensified naval and police patrols. Although Malaysia and Singapore have increased their enforcement effectiveness in recent years, creating a national coast guard,[53] indigenous Southeast Asian enforcement capacity alone is still generally insufficient to combat the problem. Air surveillance and pursuit would be an important adjunct, but most Southeast Asian nations, and particularly Indonesia, the locus of many of the incidents, do not have and cannot afford the number of aircraft necessary to adequately patrol their vast coastal region. International assistance in developing the indigenous patrol capacity of Southeast Asian maritime nations is a long-term solution to promoting regional security and would minimize the sensitive presence of foreign naval vessels.

Agreements made in 1992 between Indonesia, Malaysia, and Singapore provided for joint anti-piracy patrols and information sharing. The 1992 Indonesia/Malaysia agreement established a Maritime Operation Planning Team to carry out co-ordinated anti-piracy patrols of the Malacca Strait. And a 1994 memorandum of understanding between Malaysia and the Philippines was aimed at co-ordinating anti-piracy patrols and sharing intelligence gathered from those patrols.[54] But these agreements were insufficient deterrents because they stopped short of actually allowing hot pursuit of pirates into a neighbour's territorial waters. The Malaysian Maritime Enforcement Co-ordination Centre stated: "Under no circumstances would we intrude into each other's territory. If we chase a ship and it runs into the other side, we let the authorities there handle it".[55] At present, there is only a "hand off" protocol in hot pursuit situations between Indonesia and Malaysia. Thus while these cooperative efforts are to be commended, and are credited with constraining the growth of piracy during much of the 1990's,[56] they also highlight the continuing difficulties of pursuing criminals across international maritime borders. Ultimately, such hot pursuit of pirates across borders will be necessary to fully address the problem.

Multilateral initiatives to address these issues have thus far been almost absent, or like the SUA Convention, raised more concerns than they addressed. However, the recently announced joint information sharing initiative concerning terrorism between the members of the Five Power Defence Arrangement of Malaysia, Australia, Great Britain, Singapore, and New Zealand may prove effective to combat both terrorism and piracy.[57] Also the Philippines, Malaysia, and Indonesia are now co-ordinating their anti-terrorism maritime patrols. And there is increased sharing of resources and co-operative training among Southeast Asian countries in mine counter-measures. This is particularly important given the vulnerability of the region's narrow straits to mines. Also, the opening of an anti-terrorism centre in Malaysia provides an opportunity to co-ordinate/co-operate with the anti-piracy centre there focused on Southeast Asia.[58] Also, commercial vessels can protect themselves by employing Ship Loc locational devices,[59] electric fences,[60] high pressure hoses,[61] security lights,[62] and pirate watches,[63] although these devices may be too expensive for small coastal trading vessels.

Recognizing the severity of the problems, the ASEAN Regional Forum (ARF) has taken a collective step towards combating piracy and other threats to maritime security in the Asia-Pacific region.[64] On 19 June 2003 the ARF issued a Statement on Co-operation Against Piracy and Other Threats to Maritime Security.

The ARF Statement was based on certain shared assumptions. The participant states and the organizations recognized that piracy and armed robbery against ships and the potential for terrorist attacks on vulnerable sea shipping threaten the Asia-Pacific region and the stability of global commerce and that regional co-operation efforts were necessary to combat transnational organized crime. Such co-operation includes co-ordination among naval and coast guard units, law enforcement agencies, shipping companies, and port authorities. Conflating the response against piracy and terrorism, the Statement proclaimed, accepted that national, regional, and international efforts to combat terrorism also enhanced the ability to combat transnational organized crime and armed robberies against ships. This has added a new security dimension to what had been traditionally viewed as criminal acts at sea.

More specifically, the ARF participants committed to undertake a series of measures to deal with the "increasingly violent international crime" of piracy and armed robbery against ships. Some of the measures can be implemented right away, such as encouraging bilateral and multilateral co-operation among ARF members, including personnel contacts, information exchanges, and anti-piracy exercises. In particular the countries will enhance their ability to share information internally and internationally; institute regional co-operation and training in anti-piracy and security measures; co-operate with the World Maritime University (under IMO) in education and training of personnel in anti-piracy and security; and provide technical assistance and capacity-building to countries that need help in developing laws, extending training, and providing equipment.

The ARF participants also endorsed ongoing efforts to establish a legal framework for regional co-operation to combat piracy and armed robberies against ships, and to consider proposals to have prescribed traffic lanes for large super tankers with coast guard or naval escorts, wherever possible, on the high seas.

However, there are some important qualifications in the ARF approach. Co-operation would be on the basis of voluntary participation and must respect territorial integrity, sovereignty, sovereign rights and national jurisdictions. Also nothing in the statement, nor any action carried out in pursuance of it, prejudices the position of ARF countries with regard to any unsettled dispute concerning sovereign or other rights over territory. Moreover, the statement does not spell out the mechanisms and processes to implement the anti-piracy measures, beyond working individually with existing institutions like IMO and IMB. Sceptics may say the ARF Statement merely sets out the measures already being undertaken by countries in the region or puts together a list of good intentions, which may not be translated into action. And the qualifications about sovereignty and jurisdiction could place limits on the potential effectiveness of collective actions against piracy and even terrorism.

For the Malacca Strait, the three Strait states and the principal users could enter an agreement under Article 43 of the 1982 UNCLOS to co-operate by securing the obligation of Strait states to suppress and prevent piracy and terrorist attacks on vessels in the Strait and the obligation of user states to provide the Strait states with the technology, equipment, and training to do so.[65] Indeed, the relevant ministers of the three Strait

States have agreed to seek financial support to enhance security in the Strait.[66]

On 22 to 26 July 2003, officials from 16 Asian countries including China, Japan, and Indonesia, convened in Seoul to discuss joint measures against maritime piracy in the region.[67] Participants discussed a possible treaty to increase anti-piracy co-operation. The Treaty would establish a joint Information Sharing Centre that provides maritime law enforcement authorities with information necessary to quickly respond to piratical acts. Extradition was also discussed.

Conclusions

The objectives of piracy and terrorism are usually different. The motivation for piracy is economic while that for terrorism is predominantly political and religious ideology.[68] Yet the conflation of piracy and terrorism has been encouraged by the fact that the motivation of the offender is irrelevant under the SUA Convention, that both piracy and terrorism occasionally use similar tactics (ship hijacking), the similar political and economic circumstances under which both piracy and terrorism tend to thrive, and the responses of the United States. On the one hand this conflation may enhance co-operation of indigenous states in prevention efforts. But on the other hand, their different perspectives on "terrorism" and sovereignty may undermine such co-operation.

Although the indigenous capacity in Southeast Asia is insufficient to combat the problem, naval patrols by outside maritime powers or even "neutral" flags are perceived as a challenge to national sovereignty. Moreover, sovereignty concerns and the ASEAN tradition of "non-interference" in internal affairs account for the reluctance of many Southeast Asian nations to ratify the 1988 Rome Convention. Naval patrols by India and the United States in the Malacca Strait may be perceived in Southeast Asia as part of a much broader regional security plan whose scope goes well beyond combating piracy and terrorist threats in the Strait. Japanese proposals for similar joint patrols have also raised suspicion of "ulterior motives." And the US-led Proliferation Security Initiative has created considerable political stress and nervousness in the region.

Furthermore, the practical effectiveness of US or Japan-led patrols is questionable. The arrest authority of foreign naval vessels exercising rights of transit through international straits is unclear. Beyond this legal jurisdictional issue, the sheer size of the vessels used, while menacing, may actually inhibit their effectiveness in pursuing pirates and would-be terrorists using small high-speed craft who have intimate knowledge of the surrounding waters. Moreover, traditionally, it is not the role of the military to function as police. The US Coast Guard might be a more acceptable and effective substitute.[69]

Because of the overlap in operational similarities, short-term countermeasures such as enhanced patrols, intelligence sharing and co-ordination, as well as ship defense will be useful for countering both piracy and terrorism. But long-term solutions aimed at eliminating the root causes of piracy and terrorism may have to be fitted to the particular problem.

To attack the problem of piracy at its root, there should be more concerted efforts at assisting both state economic development and maritime enforcement capacity building in Southeast Asia. Indeed, piracy is largely driven by poor economic conditions, and by addressing that issue, a major cause of piracy can also be addressed. However, the organized crime syndicates responsible for major ship hijackings such as the *Alondra Rainbow*, may not be curtailed by economic development, because the potential returns of hijacking are so high. Thus these "high end" criminals must be denied bases and the transnational criminal networks that enable syndicates to transfer stolen cargo and ships must be disrupted. Also by promoting state development efforts, and assisting the building and strengthening of coast guards and internal security and intelligence capacity, these crime syndicates may be dealt with more effectively.

Addressing the threat of terrorism *qua* terrorism is more problematic, and involves more complicated and sensitive questions of religion, ideology, sovereignty, and foreign policy. It should be remembered that although ship hijacking or attack by terrorists in Southeast Asia is a serious potential threat, it is so far just that and not yet a reality. Perhaps standard anti-terrorist approaches such as disrupting the finances and leadership of the sponsoring organization may be effective in the short term. But by helping these states develop their own surveillance and enforcement capacities, long term, and longer lasting, solutions will be possible. A relevant example may be the US project to create a Yemeni coast guard complete with high-tech equipped gunboats and training.[70] Ultimately, however, some nations may have to provide greater cultural and religious "space" for dissident groups. Thus to combat the threat of piracy and maritime terrorism, both indigenous countries and external maritime powers should focus on what has created the threat, rather than its symptoms.

Notes

1 This chapter uses excerpts from Adam Young and Mark J. Valencia, "Conflation of Piracy and Terrorism in Southeast Asia: Rectitude and Utility", *Contemporary Southeast Asia* 25, no. 2 (August 2003): 269–83.

2 Keith Bradsher, "Attacks on Chemical Ships in Southeast Asia Seem to be Piracy, Not Terror", *New York Times*, 27 March 2003.

3 Marcus Hand, "Piracy Attacks on Three Chemical Tankers Bring Fears of Terrorism Dry Runs", *Lloyd's List*, 31 March 2003.

4 Richard Halloran, "What if Asia's Pirates and Terrorists Joined Hands?" *South China Morning Post*, 17 May 2003; Anonymous, "China Gives 'Guarded' Response to Indian Warships in Malacca Strait", *BBC Monitoring International Reports*, 18 July 2002; Sea Lanes, Oil Rigs a "Terror Target", *CNN.com*, 19 September 2002; "Piracy Watchdog Points Finger at Aceh Separatists", *Straits Times Interactive News*, 4 February 2002; Bhagyashree Garekar, "Piracy in Malacca Strait Linked to Indonesia's Instability", *Straits Times*, 27 January 2003; David Osler, "Target: Tankers", *Lloyd's List*, 6 February 2003.

5 Vivian Ho, "No Let Down in Global Attacks by Pirates", *Kyodo News Service*, 24 July 2003.

6 Samuel Pyeatt Menefee, "Crossing the Line?" in *Combating Piracy and Ship Robbery*, edited by Hamzah Ahmad and Akira Ogawa (Tokyo: Okazaki Institute, 2001), pp. 61–62; United Nations, *Official Text of the United Nations Convention on the Law of the Sea* (New York: United Nations, 1983), Article 101; United Nations, Convention on the High Seas (1958), *United Nations Treaty Series* (New York: United Nations, 1963), no. 6465, vol. 450, pp. 82–103.

7 Menefee, op. cit.

8 International Maritime Organization, *Draft Code of Practice for the Investigation of the Crimes of Piracy and Armed Robbery Against Ships*. MSC/Circ 984, 20 December 2000.

9 Samuel Pyeatt Menefee, "Terrorism at Sea: The Historical Development of an International Legal Response" in *Violence at Sea*, edited by Brian A.H. Parritt (Paris: CBE, 1986), p. 192.

10 Ibid.

11 Tina Garmon, "Comment: International Law of the Sea: Reconciling the Law of Piracy and Terrorism in the Wake of September 11th", *The Maritime Lawyer*, Winter, 2002.

[12]   Natalino Ronzitti, "The Law of the Sea and the Use of Force Against Terrorist
       Activities" in *Maritime Terrorism and International Law*, edited by Natalino Ronzitti
       (Dordrecht: Martinus Nijhoff, 1990).

[13]   Young and Valencia, op. cit.

[14]   Peter Chalk, "Contemporary Maritime Piracy in Southeast Asia", *Studies in
       Conflict and Terrorism*, 16 March 21 1997, vol. 21: p. 89.

[15]   IMB statistics found in: Stanley Weeks, "Piracy and Regional Security" in
       Combating Piracy and Ship Robber, edited by Hamzah Ahmad and Akira Ogawa
       (Tokyo: Okazaki Institute, 2001), p. 92.

[16]   Incident related in Jayant Abhyankar, "Piracy and Ship Robbery: A Growing
       Menace" in *Combating Piracy and Ship Robbery*, edited by Hamzah Ahmad and
       Akira Ogawa (Tokyo: Okazaki Institute, 2001), p. 25.

[17]   Ibid., pp. 29–30.

[18]   Ibid., pp. 30–31.

[19]   Ibid., p. 31.

[20]   Chalk, op. cit., p. 93.

[21]   Eric Watkins, "US Offer of Escorts and Risk Cover Greeted with Skepticism",
       Lloyd's List, 27 March 2003.

[22]   Anonymous, "US Interdiction Poses Legal Problems", *Oxford Analytica*,
       30 June 2003.

[23]   J. Ashley Roach, "United States Initiatives to Enhance Maritime Security at
       Sea" in *Marine Policy* (Special Issue, edited by Mark J. Valencia and Kazumine
       Akimoto) 28, no. 1 (January 2004): 3.

[24]   Anonymous, "US Interdiction Poses Legal Problems", *Oxford Analytica*,
       30 June 2003.

[25]   David Osler, "Target: Tankers", *Lloyd's List*, 6 February 2003.

[26]   Eric Watkins, "Security — Al-Qa'eda Suspect Admits Role in Limburg", *Lloyd's
       List*, 21 January 2003.

[27]   Jeffrey D. Simon, "The Implications of the Achille Lauro Hijacking for the
       Maritime Community" in *Violence at Sea*, edited by Brian A.H. Parritt (Paris:
       CBE, 1986), pp. 18–19.

[28]   Ibid., p. 19.

[29]   <http://www.ict.org.il/spotlight/det.cfm?id=837>; sources: *Associated Press,
       BBC News, Reuters,* the *Times of India*; Anonymous, "Crime — Piracy Soars to
       Record Level", *Lloyd's List*, 2 May 2003.

[30]   Ho, op. cit.

[31]   Anonymous, "Piracy Watchdog Points Finger at Aceh Separatists", *Straits
       Times Interactive News*, 4 February 2002; Anonymous, "China Gives "Guarded"
       Response to Indian Warships in Malacca Strait", *BBC Monitoring International
       Reports*, 18 July 2002.

[32] Convention for the Supression of Unlawful Acts Against the Safety of Maritime Navigation, 1988, <http://www.imo.org/conventions/contents.asp?topic_id=259&doc_id=686>.

[33] Roach, op. cit., p. 26.

[34] Jay L. Batongbacal, "Trends in Anti-piracy Co-operation in the ASEAN Region" in *Combating Piracy and Ship Robbery*, edited by Hamzah Ahmad and Akira Ogawa (Tokyo: Okazaki Institute, 2001), p. 125.

[35] International Chamber of Commerce (ICC) and International Maritime Bureau (IMB), Piracy Report, <http://www.iccwbo.org/home/news_archives/2002/stories/piracy%20report%20Oct2002.asp>; Roach, *op. cit.*, p. 3.

[36] Anonymous, "SUA Review Continues as Legal Experts Tackle Security", *IMO News,* no. 4 (2002), pp. 16–17.

[37] Anonymous, "Experts Want Force to Pursue Pirates", *Lloyd's List*, 28 February 2002; Marcus Hand, "Security — Co-operation Call to Ward off Malacca Strait Attacks", *Lloyd's List*, 20 February 2003.

[38] Hugh O'Mahony, "Greenpeace Hijacks Tanker in Turkey", *Lloyd's List*, 8 July 2002.

[39] Michael Evans, "US Plans to Seize Suspects At Will", *The Times* (London), 11 July 2003.

[40] Charles Dragonette, *"Office of Naval Intelligence Analysis Department Worldwide Threat to Shipping Mariner Warning Information"*, 21 February 2002.

[41] Sudha Ramachandran, "India Signs on as Southeast Asia Watchdog", *Asia Times Online*, 5 April 2002.

[42] Donald Urquhart, "Japan Helping Indonesia Set Up Coast Guard", *Business Times Singapore*, 25 March 2003.

[43] Chalk, op. cit., p. 96.

[44] Anonymous, "Asia US Initiative Sets Stage for Miscalculations, Clashes?", *Stratfor*, 8 July 2003.

[45] David Sanger and Thom Shanker, "Reluctant US Gives Assent for Missiles to Go to Yemen", *New York Times*, 12 December 2002, pp. A1 and A20.

[46] Brendan Pearson, "Tokyo Treads Warily on Use of Interdiction Force", *Australian Financial Review*, 12 July 2003; Takashi Ono and Yoshiro Mino, "Japan Nervous as Star of WMD Exercise", *The Asahi Shimbun*, 15 September 2003.

[47] Anonymous, "Asian Nations Begin Talks in Japan on Measures to Combat Maritime Piracy", *BBC Monitoring Asia Pacific-Political*, London, 12 March 2002.

[48] Anonymous, "Brunei: Hijack Drama on High Seas", *Borneo Bulletin*, 15 August 2002.

[49] Anonymous, "Japan to Send Coast Guard Boat on Anti Terrorist Mission", *BBC Monitoring Asia Pacific-Political*, London, 18 October 2002.

50   Anonymous, "Philippines, Japan Lead Multilateral Anti-Piracy Exercises", *BBC Monitoring Asia-Pacific-Political*, London, 7 March 2003.

51   Donald Urquhart, "Malaysia Acts to Create National Coast Guard, IN Will Use the Japan Coast Guard as its Model", *Business Times Singapore*, 8 July 2003.

52   David Boey, "Navy Takes the Rough with the Smooth", *Straits Times*, 5 May 2003.

53   Ibid.

54   Ibid.

55   Quoted in Chalk, op. cit., p. 100.

56   Ibid., p. 99.

57   *Reuters* in the Online *Washington Post*, <http://www.washingtonpost.com/wp-dyn/articles/A47738-2003Apr28.html>.

58   Anonymous, "Ports World, Malaysia Hopes to Host a New Anti-Piracy Centre", *New Straits Times*, 14 April 2003.

59   Peter Hadfield, "Repel Boarders", *New Scientist*, v. 167 (12 August 2000), p. 14; Abhyankar, op. cit., p. 48.

60   ICC-IMB website, "Pirate Attacks Against Ships Increase, ICC Report Finds".

61   Batongbacal, op. cit., p. 109; Chalk, op. cit., p. 97.

62   Abhyankar, op. cit., p. 43.

63   ICC-IMB website. "High Seas Terrorism Alert in Piracy Report". <http://www.iccwbo.org/home/news_archives/2003/stories/piracy%20_report 2002.asp>; Abhyankar, op. cit., p. 43; Batongbacal, op. cit., p. 108; Chalk, op. cit., p. 97.

64   Mohamed Ali, "Maritime Security Co-operation the ARF Way", 10 July 2003.

65   Marcus Hand, "Security — Co-operation Call to Ward Off Malacca Strait Attacks", *Lloyd's List*, 20 February 2003.

66   David Osler, "Malacca Strait Security on Agenda", *Lloyd's List*, 23 September 2002.

67   Anonymous, "Anti-Piracy Conference Opens in Seoul", *Asian Pulse*, 22 July 2003.

68   There are no hard and fast lines separating economic and political motives, for one can often support the other, but the vast majority of pirates are not politically motivated.

69   Bruce B. Stubbs, "Piracy and Terrorism", *The Washington Times*, Letters, 10 July 2003.

70   Jerry Frank, "Washington Backs Yemen in Piracy and Terrorism Fight", *Lloyd's List*, 21 August 2002.

5

Piracy and Politics in Southeast Asia[1]

Mark J. Valencia

Introduction: The Problem

Piracy in Southeast Asia is posing political dilemmas for policymakers. Piracy incidents in and around the Straits of Malacca and Singapore have increased at an alarming rate — in both number and severity. In 2003, more than 40 per cent of the world's 445 incidents of piracy were in Southeast Asia, particularly in the Malacca/Singapore Straits and Indonesian waters, which, with 121 attacks became the world's most piracy-prone area.[2] Although most of these "piracy" acts occurred in ports or anchorages,[3] others involved "shipjacking" and the murder of the crew. These modern pirates are increasingly a far cry from the swashbuckling rouges of old. Although many incidents do involve simple robbery of the crew and the contents of the ship's safe, others are often fomented by organized international gangs which plan the crime well in advance, hijack the ship with its cargo and sell both in foreign markets. And even the so-called "simple" robberies often involve tying or locking up the entire crew, which means the ship is steaming ahead unmanned. These criminals are often violent and are increasingly targeting ships and citizens of maritime powers like Japan.

In response, the maritime powers, particularly Japan which depends on the sea-lanes through the Straits for much of its oil imports, have raised a hue and cry for immediate and effective action to make the seas "safe" for navigation. Japan has even publicly proposed a regional coast guard to combat the problem (See Chaikin, this volume). But this increasing public pressure on the coastal states, as well as proposals by maritime powers for their own involvement in piracy suppression, have raised old and new political questions.

Indigenous Efforts

Indigenous regional co-operation between anti-piracy enforcement agencies began in 1992 when the Regional Piracy Centre was established in Kuala Lumpur with the support of the shipping industry, the International Maritime Organization (IMO), and law enforcement agencies to provide a central information reporting and warning centre for the area between Sri Lanka and Northeast Asia. In October 2003, the leaders of the Association of Southeast Asian Nations (ASEAN) pledged to strengthen ties to counter terrorism, piracy, and other transnational crimes through creation of a "security" community.[4] And the ASEAN Ministers meeting in January 2004 considered the progress of the ASEAN action plan to combat piracy.[5] Even China and ASEAN issued a joint declaration on co-operation against piracy, among others.[6]

There are also numerous bilateral agreements to control piracy. There are parallel agreements among Singapore, Indonesia, and Malaysia to *co-ordinate* naval patrols and conduct periodic anti-piracy exercises in the Malacca and Singapore Straits. These patrols supposedly were the cause of an almost complete reduction of piracy attacks in the Straits for several years. Although the number of incidents rose again, Indonesia/ Malaysia co-operation in the Strait of Malacca again supposedly resulted in a decrease of piracy incidents from 44 in 2001 to 21 in 2003.[7] Moreover, Indonesia and Malaysia signed an Incidents at Sea Agreement which could serve as a model or even be expanded to include others. And the Philippines and Malaysia have been undertaking co-ordinated border patrol exercises for sometime.[8]

With all this supposed effort, both regionally and bilaterally, it would seem that piracy and its perpetrators would sharply decrease if not disappear. But in fact, piracy in the region is on the increase — in both frequency and degree of violence[9] — and it is now obvious that Southeast Asian responses and indigenous capabilities are no longer adequate to address the problem. Why is this so?

Clearly some of these co-operative "activities" are little more than "talk shops" that lead to little action or implementation of the ideas that are discussed. But there are more concrete reasons for the failure to suppress piracy. Almost everybody acknowledges that the core of the problem is in Indonesia,[10] where the general breakdown of order, the growth of corruption[11] and an apparent lack of will and resources to tackle the problem appear to be the main factors in the rise in Southeast Asian piracy. Increased poverty and higher unemployment have also helped make piracy an attractive source of income. Indonesian defence spending has decreased by 65 per cent, and maritime forces are already stretched thin because of communal and ethnic unrest in the Moluccas, Irian Jaya, and Aceh.[12] The Indonesian Navy only has about 115 ships that can patrol about a third of the country's waters.[13] And the Navy has just moved some of its warships to offshore Aceh to blockade the area to prevent arms smuggling.[14]

In an attempt to demonstrate its concern, Indonesia replaced its Western Fleet Sea Security Task Force Commander because of his inability to control piracy in his area. However, corruption among poorly paid maritime officials and port workers enable the transfer of information to pirates concerning the movements of ships and the composition of their cargo. Moreover, maritime security forces are proving to be no match for well-organized pirates, who use radar to locate vessels, gather intelligence from radio transmissions and informers, carry out their attacks using motorized boats and automatic weapons, and easily escape in boats that blend in with the hundreds of small ships sailing in the area. Given the serious problems of poverty and secessionist movements, piracy of other countries' ships is simply not a current priority for the Indonesian government. Thus the problem is more fundamental and requires longer-term, broad-based economic development.

Although Singapore and other neighbours might be of assistance to Indonesia, the ASEAN policy of non-interference in the domestic affairs of member states has hindered co-ordinated efforts to combat piracy. Indeed many member countries are unwilling to prosecute pirates in their own territorial waters for acts of piracy committed under another country's jurisdiction.

Japan's Role

This general lack of an adequate indigenous response has provided an opportunity for leadership by Japan which has had more than 140 of its ships attacked over the past eleven years and which depends on deliveries of Middle East oil through the Strait of Malacca.[15] Tokyo has convened several recent international conferences — the "International Conference of All Maritime Related Concerns, both Governmental and Private, on Combating Piracy and Armed Robbery Against Ships," from 28–30 March 2000, which issued the "Tokyo Appeal" for action, and the 27–29 April 2000 "Asia Anti-Piracy Challenges 2000: Regional Conference on Combating Piracy and Armed Robbery Against Ships," which consisted of Heads of Coast Guard Agencies of fifteen countries ranging from India to Japan. The April 2000 intergovernmental agreement promotes mutual co-operation against piracy/sea robbery through enhanced information exchange, reports, law enforcement activities, investigations, and Japanese support for training and technology. And a series of Expert Meetings on Combating Piracy and Armed Robbery were held in Tokyo (2000), Bangkok (2001), Kuala Lumpur (2002) and Manila (2003), organized by the Japan Coast Guard (JCG) and supported by the Nippon Foundation. In September 2003, sixteen nations met in Tokyo at the fifth such meeting and finalized a draft of an anti-piracy pact.[16] These meetings evaluated joint patrol exercises and assisted in the development of equipment and materials, and improving information networks.

Japan has also provided a concrete presence and assistance. In November 2000, Japan held joint patrols with India and Malaysia.[17] In 2001, the JCG visited Singapore, the Philippines, and Thailand and JCG aircraft were sent to Thailand and the Philippines as part of the JCG's anti-piracy programme. In 2002 JCG patrol vessels visited Brunei, Indonesia, the Philippines, Vietnam, Malaysia, and Singapore.[18] And Vietnam and Japan have pledged to broaden military co-operation in preventing piracy.[19] In February 2004, the JCG vessel Ryukyu was dispatched to participate in anti-piracy exercises with Thailand and the Philippines.[20] And perhaps most significant of all, in November 2003, it was announced that Japan would send a patrol vessel to Singapore to take part in anti-piracy drills and *actual patrolling*.[21]

The Ministry of Foreign Affairs (MOFA) is a significant broker in developing Japan's counter-piracy efforts. MOFA's policies to promote co-operation among Asian countries in the battle against piracy are:

"1. to examine and follow-up regional co-operation agreements on anti-piracy measures;
2. to raise the profile of the "piracy problem" at international meetings such as ASEAN+3 and encourage regional countries to become signatories to the Rome Convention like Brunei, the Philippines, Singapore and Vietnam have recently done;[22]
3. to support poverty counter-measures in areas where piratical attacks occur frequently;
4. to support the development of coast guard agencies, focusing on human resources development and technical assistance; and
5. to support ship industry activities that promote ship and port security".[23]

Japan's counter-piracy initiatives have had some successes in terms of aiding indigenous efforts. The Indonesian government has accepted Japanese technical and financial assistance in creating a coast guard. And in March 2003 senior officials from the Indonesian Ministry of National Development Planning, the Marine and Air Police and the Directorate General of Sea Communications visited Japan to study JCG operations. The Indonesian Marine and Air Police and the Directorate General of Sea Communications will be merged into a newly established Indonesian Coast Guard (ICG). If the ICG becomes a reality, a number of countries including the United States have offered vessels and financial assistance.[24] Malaysia is also considering the consolidation of its eleven maritime law enforcement agencies into a Malaysian Coast Guard and the JCG has been mooted as the desired model.[25] These developments suggest a shift from confidence building measures to increasing levels of co-operation and more vigorous individual state action to fight maritime piracy.

Lessons from Northeast Asia

In Northeast Asia, piracy has also been an impediment to safe navigation for commercial vessels.[26] From 1992, piracy in the East China Sea took on a more overt, quasi-military quality, with Chinese attackers in uniform and in government patrol boats, often firing weapons. Between 1991 and 1992, there were 78 such incidents. Beijing eventually claimed that rogue elements of the Chinese Customs and Public Security Bureaus were responsible.

After 17 piracy incidents involving Russian ships in the East China Sea over several years, in mid-1993, Moscow deployed naval vessels to the area with orders to attack any threats to shipping. The incidents promptly ceased. Japan, whose ships were also victims, proposed to then Chinese Foreign Minister Qian Qichen during his February 1993 visit to Tokyo that officials from the two countries' coastguard authorities should meet to discuss East China Sea shipping problems. Beijing agreed to an "informal" June 1993 meeting, which established a "hotline" to the JCG. Over the next year, such incidents were reduced to one.

These countries were successful in stemming piracy because:

1.   the incidents were occurring on the high seas so there was no question of sovereignty regarding the involvement of foreign warships;
2.   Russia took a prompt and forceful approach;
3.   China was apparently able to exert domestic control over the perpetrators; and
4.   the victim countries and the source country established good communication to address the problem.

None of these factors exist in Southeast Asia.

Political Obstacles to Co-operation

If the coastal states cannot control piracy either individually or together, why will they not invite or allow outside powers to do so? The reasons include sovereignty concerns and jurisdictional uncertainty — nationally as well as domestically.

Almost all acts of piracy in or near the Straits of Malacca and Singapore occur in the territorial or archipelagic waters of Malaysia, Indonesia, or Singapore.[27] And acts of piracy in Indonesia are mostly within its archipelagic and territorial waters. Littoral state civil maritime law enforcement authorities (coast guards, marine police, and port police) continue to have responsibility for preventing or responding to sea robbery in ports and territorial waters. Under universally accepted international law, law enforcement officials may not enforce their laws in areas under the territorial sovereignty of another state. Therefore, naval vessels or marine police from one state may not — without permission — enter the internal, territorial, or archipelagic waters of another state to patrol for pirates or to arrest persons for acts of piracy, regardless of where such acts took place.

Further, ever since the US-led unilateral interventions in Kosovo and Iraq, sovereignty is no longer a theoretical concern. Indeed some smaller countries view it as the last defence against bullying by bigger powers. Perhaps Japan and the United States could better understand this concern if they considered the issue in relation to their insistence on absolute, unadulterated freedom of navigation in EEZs or unimpeded "transit passage" in straits used for international navigation. Indonesia and Malaysia are faced with an increasing intensity and severity of major oil spills from foreign tankers in the Malacca Strait as well as the possibility of catastrophic accidents involving carriers of ultrahazardous cargoes including plutonium which may pass through the Strait. In response they have repeatedly tried to persuade the maritime powers, particularly Japan and the United States, to agree to a stricter regime for such vessels in the Straits. But this has been strongly and successfully resisted by the maritime powers because they will not allow the concept of freedom of navigation to be eroded in any way. Thus Indonesia and Malaysia jealously guard what is left of their maritime "sovereignty".[28]

Another obstacle to co-operation is that jurisdiction over piracy is uncertain in disputed maritime areas in some parts of the southern Malacca and Singapore Straits and in a large area of multiple claims in the South China Sea where boundaries have not been agreed. In light of these legal constraints and uncertainties, there is a clear need for transborder bilateral and multilateral co-operation to effectively deal with piracy.

The Politics of Possible Responses

There are several possible responses to the piracy problem in Southeast Asia: extraregional and/or regional government to government joint patrols; training and technical assistance from the maritime powers; and private sector initiatives like emplacing concealed transponders on ships, reporting fully and promptly all piracy incidents to the International Maritime Bureau, capacity building, and employing armed guards on commercial vessels.

There are serious problems for government to government joint patrols. First of all, the governments concerned cannot agree on the definition of piracy. And the Southeast Asian states oppose a definition that would allow foreign coast guard or naval vessels into their waters. Second, some Southeast Asian countries like Indonesia cannot agree internally on who should have or has jurisdiction over this issue — the navy or the coast guard. Third, the coastal states and the maritime powers cannot agree on whose problem piracy is, and for all these reasons they cannot agree on which country or countries should take the lead in enforcement in the region.

A co-operative anti-piracy initiative — a regional coast guard — was proposed in November 1999 to Japanese Prime Minister Keizo Obuchi at the summit meeting in Manila of ASEAN heads of government.[29] But bitter memories in the region of Japan's brutal wartime occupation, and domestic resistance in Japan to a foreign military role are major obstacles to carrying out the proposal. China has been reticent about co-operating on regional security measures thus leaving the door open for Japan. Indeed, some analysts view the proposal as an attempt by Japan to reassert its waning influence in the region as a counterbalance to China.[30] Moreover, some think Tokyo sees the move as a way of delicately distinguishing itself and its approach from that of the United States. The initiative could be part of a broader strategy developed at Japan's National Institute for Defence Studies. Such a strategy envisages a Japan-led international Ocean Peacekeeping Force, which would be primarily concerned with activities that are necessary to fulfil obligations under the 1982 UN Convention on the Law of the Sea to maintain maritime order and prevent armed conflict at sea.

Such a Force would conduct joint monitoring activities to protect the environment and resources in waters beyond state control, as well as combat illegal activities that span international maritime boundaries, including illegal fishing, illegal entry and piracy. It would have both "benign" military duties, such as search and rescue, and constabulary functions. There have been many examples of bilateral co-operation of this type — the United States and Russia in the Bering Sea, for instance, and Indonesia and Malaysia, and Indonesia and Singapore, in the Strait of Malacca — but none on a multilateral basis. The long-term vision has the peacekeeping force providing a framework for security co-operation between Japan, the United States, China, and Russia.

To avoid a dominant and objectionable presence, Japan proposed that its ships which would be participating in the multilateral anti-piracy force be drawn from its civilian-controlled coast guard, rather than from its navy. And Tokyo has suggested that other participants in the force include China, South Korea, Indonesia, Malaysia, and Singapore. The response from some Southeast Asian countries to the proposed anti-piracy initiative was initially favourable.

But China opposed the proposal from the very beginning, perhaps because it sees the Japanese proposal as an attempt to pre-empt China's emergence as the dominant power in Asia. And now Malaysia and Indonesia have clarified that they are unwilling to allow foreign-armed vessels into their territorial waters.[31] Joint exercises and training are acceptable to them, but not actual joint patrols.

This is why Japan's primary effort has turned to building indigenous capacity. The April 2000 Tokyo meeting addressed the problem on two levels: information exchange and co-operation among national coast guard agencies; and a policy conference of senior maritime officials. The meeting adopted a declaration on measures to be taken against piracy in Asia. To apply these measures, Japan offered to help countries with weak maritime surveillance capabilities by providing experts and training staff. It is the latter that interests the ASEAN nations the most.

Although it is clear that leadership is needed from Asia's two largest powers, Japan and/or China, mistrust of Japan has made China and other possible partners reluctant to accept Japan's initiative for joint patrols. Another significant problem for Japan is that under the current interpretation of Article 9 of its Constitution, its coast guard can only use force if the vessel being attacked is Japanese. That obviously would not make Japan a very effective partner in an international coast guard.[32]

Thus regarding Japan's possible role in a "joint coast guard", there are several important but as yet unanswered questions. Is a leadership role for Japan acceptable to the region, and domestically, given the fears of the region and domestic sensitivity to a foreign Japanese "military" presence?

If it is to be a leader, where will it focus its effort and what exactly can and will it do? Clearly controversy will increase as Japan extends its defence perimeter further away from its territorial waters.

Thinking outside the box, perhaps China could take the lead. However, its aggressive behaviour regarding its claims to disputed islands in the region and its unwillingness to sign a formal code of conduct for the South China Sea that would permanently defuse tensions there have scared off potential partners. Moreover, China strongly prefers bilateral over multilateral co-operation so that it can better "manage" the relationship. And would China be willing to lead, and if not, will it participate at all in any multilateral effort? And if it does not, can any such effort be effective?

What about the United States in a leadership role in this sector? The United States wants China to join international civil society and may see this as an opportunity to draw China into a system of reducing tensions and solving disputes. Then US Commander-in-Chief for the Pacific Admiral Dennis Blair cited anti-piracy as one of the common interests in his bid to shift the American emphasis from bilateral security treaties to multilateral security communities.[33] It was thought that China's participation in such communities might help ease its fears of US intentions in the region and earn it some trust and gratitude from its neighbours.

The United States also proposed an Asia-Pacific Regional Initiative, built upon US bilateral arrangements with several countries in the region. Admiral Blair thought that the joint US-Thailand military exercise known as Cobra Gold[34] was a good model to build on for future multilateral security co-operation in the region. While originally a bilateral affair, Cobra Gold, held since 1982, recently has drawn interest of other countries, including Singapore, Malaysia, and Australia which have expressed a desire to participate in future exercises. Admiral Blair said that he hoped that the joint US-Philippine "Balikatan" military exercise under both countries' Visiting Forces Agreement would be "linked" to the Cobra Gold initiative so more governments in the region could undertake joint training of their armed forces. During the 2003 Cobra Gold exercise, Thailand reportedly invited China, which sent its military attaché to observe the event.

But is the US proposal for multilateral naval exercises acceptable to the region? Or will it stimulate controversy and even tension between US allies (Japan, South Korea, the Philippines, and Thailand) and other Asian states more concerned with China's negative reaction to this bold initiative?

For example, the Philippines was initially reluctant to participate in US-led multilateral exercises with Thailand, Singapore, and Australia for fear of antagonizing China. Indeed, it was an effort to allay China's concern that resulted in the Philippines inviting China to observe its Balikatan bilateral exercises with the United States. And Beijing expressed concern over trilateral US-Philippine-Thai naval exercises held 21–23 March 2001 near Scarborough Shoal. Moreover, China refused to participate in a meeting of coast guard officials from the United States, Japan, South Korea, and Russia convened in Tokyo on 20–21 December 2000,[35] and again in Vladivostok on 14 March 2001, to discuss anti-piracy and drug and gun smuggling prevention in the northwestern Pacific. Nevertheless, if this latter initiative is successful, it could form the core of an eventual broader multinational approach.

Conflation of Piracy and Terrorism

There has been a conscious attempt to conflate piracy and terrorism in Southeast Asia. Singapore has been the leading voice in this public campaign.[36] Indeed Singapore is concerned that terrorists may disguise themselves as pirates and therefore wants pirates treated as terrorists. It is particularly worried that a terrorist act in the narrow Malacca/Singapore Straits or in its port could impede traffic and or raise insurance rates causing traffic to detour around the Straits and Singapore itself. This would not only raise freight rates worldwide but also damage Singapore's economy which depends to a large degree on servicing such ships and refining their crude oil. By conflating the two phenomena it apparently hopes its maritime neighbours, Indonesia and Malaysia, will either enhance their defences or allow Singapore or a UN-sponsored task force to patrol their waters in the Straits.[37]

If piracy and terrorism are fused into a general threat, developing countries may find outside help easier to accept and to "sell" to their publics. However, evidence that the two are conflated is sketchy at best.[38] Analysts point to Al-Qaeda's announced plan to target the world economy by launching attacks against shipping in key sea-lanes of Southeast Asia.[39] And some diplomats in the region have suggested that piracy attacks in the Malacca Strait have recently increased because the Aceh Independence Movement (GAM) is in desperate need of money. When pirates kidnapped several crew members of the Penrider in the

Strait of Malacca, and held them for ransom, it was alleged by the victims that the pirates were GAM members.[40] Similar rumours attribute pirate attacks to the Abu Sayyaf movement in the southern Philippines.[41] Some speculate that terrorists are kidnapping ship's officers to learn how to drive ships and kidnapping dive instructors to learn how to carryout underwater sabotage.[42] However this is all circumstantial and speculative. What was not circumstantial or speculative however was the 27 February 2004 Abu Sayyaf-claimed bombing of a ferry two hours after it left Manila for the central and southern Philippines.[43] Whether or not terrorists are becoming pirates, such conflation could have both expected and unexpected political ramifications. For example, the United States is offering assistance to and seeking assistance from regional states to combat terrorism. If piracy were equated with terrorism this might encourage more states to accept such assistance and give permission to US forces to patrol their waters. The United States is already providing such assistance to the Philippines in its struggle with its secessionist-minded south. And it may provide Indonesia with the necessary helicopters, missile boats and patrol boats to control its waters.[44]

Similarly, India has launched an initiative to control piracy and terrorism in the outer western approaches to the Malacca Strait and in the Andaman and Nicobar islands.[45] And India and the United States have focused joint military exercises on counter-terrorism. Moreover, Indian and US naval ships conducted 24 joint missions escorting ships of high value through the Malacca Strait. The point is that if piracy becomes conflated with terrorism, this could provide an opportunity and boost for an Indian military presence in Southeast Asia. This in turn would make China, and some Southeast Asian states rather nervous.

Such appeals for action based on worst case scenarios are not confined to Singapore.[46] The International Maritime Bureau has stated that it is only a matter of time before pirates cause an environmental disaster. And the Federation of ASEAN Shipowners' Associations has appealed directly to the 10 ASEAN heads of state for action. They argue that a catastrophic incident would send a message to the world that the region is unsafe and thus have dire economic consequences. And one senior tanker industry executive has even called for the "internationalization" of the Straits of Malacca and Singapore under a UN umbrella. This is anathema for Indonesia and Malaysia.

Regional Forums: Enhancing the Epistemic Community[47]

Given that the maritime powers are struggling with the leadership question and regional states are struggling with the effectiveness of co-operation among themselves, what can be done in the meantime? The task at hand is to build an epistemic community supportive of multilateral co-operation in an anti-piracy effort. To this end Japan and ASEAN could broaden and deepen their participation in regional security fora. For example, the major forum for naval dialogue and co-operation in the region is the Western Pacific Naval Symposium (WPNS). The WPNS brings together leaders from the navies of the Western Pacific in their "unofficial" capacities to discuss issues of common concern, including law of the sea and the security of sea lines of communication (SLOCs). Its membership includes China, Japan, and South Korea from Northeast Asia, together with the navies of the ASEAN countries, Papua New Guinea, Australia, New Zealand, France, and the United States.

The main thrust of the WPNS has not been multilateral naval operations, which were considered too sensitive, but rather the harmonization of existing procedures. A tangible outcome from the WPNS meetings has been a series of subordinate workshops which have led to the development of a Maritime Information Exchange Directory, a WPNS Tactical Signals Handbook, a WPNS Replenishment at Sea Handbook, and planning for the conduct of a Command Post Exercise (CPX) to help the development of common doctrine and publications. Recent meetings of the WPNS have concentrated largely on civil responsibilities (maritime safety, search and rescue, disaster relief, and protection of the marine environment) because these were safer issues for the forum to consider. This is despite the fact that in most Asia-Pacific countries, agencies other than navies usually have responsibility for these matters.

The ASEAN Regional Forum (ARF) has also begun to discuss piracy issues. For example, an ARF Maritime Senior Officials Meeting was convened in Honolulu in November, 1999 to consider and discuss ways and means for the ARF to add value to existing activities in the areas of maritime safety, law and order at sea, and protection and preservation of the marine environment. The recommendations arising from the meeting included the control of piracy and the ratification of maritime conventions.

The recommendation was subsequently considered at a further meeting of the Inter-Sessional Support Group on Confidence Building Measures in Bangkok in March 1999 that agreed to continue considering maritime co-operation, especially in the CBM context. That meeting also agreed that anti-piracy efforts and the ratification of various maritime conventions warranted specific monitoring by the ARF.

Regarding Track 2, or informal, activities, The Council for Security Co-operation in the Asia-Pacific (CSCAP) has established a working group to look specifically at maritime security co-operation in the Asia-Pacific region. This group has adopted a broad view of security and is considering a range of small "s" security issues, such as marine safety, resource conservation, oceans governance (particularly in areas where maritime boundaries are not agreed) and unlawful activities at sea, e.g., drug smuggling, illegal population movements and *piracy*, as well as more conventional maritime security issues. A major achievement of the CSCAP Maritime Co-operation Working Group has been the development and promulgation of proposed Guidelines for Regional Maritime Co-operation.[48] These are a set of fundamental, non-binding principles to guide regional maritime co-operation and to ensure a common understanding and approach to maritime issues in the region. In addition to recognizing the general "confidence-building benefits of naval co-operation," the Guidelines support regional maritime co-operation in maritime safety (Articles 13–15), search and rescue (Articles 22, 23), marine resources (Articles 24, 25), marine scientific research (Articles 26, 27), technical co-operation and capacity-building (Article 28), and training and education (Article 29).

Next Steps

Besides more "talk," what action can be taken? One way to proceed would be for all members of ASEAN to follow the lead of Singapore, Brunei, the Philippines and Vietnam and sign the IMO's 1988 Rome Convention for the Suppression of Unlawful Acts Against the Safety of Maritime Navigation. Ratification of the Convention will make it easier for ASEAN governments to prosecute pirates, because it gives signatory governments the power — even the duty — to prosecute pirates caught in their own territorial waters for acts of piracy committed under another country's jurisdiction.

Japan and the United States can also play an important role by providing assistance to the newly established ASEAN Center for Transnational Crime and helping it develop concrete measure to fight piracy. Since Japan might have some constitutional difficulty assisting local navies, the United States could help by allowing its coast guard to train various ASEAN maritime security forces in determining and implementing appropriate measures to combat piracy. Such assistance would send a signal to Southeast Asia that the United States is committed to the region's security and economic well-being.

Conclusions

Although there seems to be quite a bit of maritime co-operation involving Asian countries and many proposals for its expansion, what is less certain is its effectiveness. Some of the co-operative "activities" have the appearance of "talk shops" that lead to little or no action. There is also a particular problem also with translating issues to an operational or practical level. Issues are often discussed at the "head office" level by senior officials with no migration of ideas to a working level.[49]

In sum, a joint patrol led by Japan, China or the United States is unlikely. Perhaps a multilateral force comprised of smaller states selected by the coastal states themselves might be possible. But in the meantime, the best bet is a combination of *ad hoc* measures — self-help by the coastal states themselves, including enhanced co-ordination and ratification of the SUA Rome Convention, and assistance from the maritime powers in training and equipment. Although some consider more talk as a poor substitute for action, over the longer term, frequent Track 2 discussions can broaden awareness of the problems and potentially identify solutions that may be too sensitive or embryonic for consideration at a "Track 1" (official) level. And such talk can help build an epistemic community supportive of the co-operative *action* needed to fight this modern day scourge of the seas.

Notes

[1]   Some of this material is excerpted or updated and revised from Mark J. Valencia, "Piracy and International Politics" in *Combating Piracy and Ship Robbery:*

Charting the Future in Asia-Pacific Waters, edited by Hamzah Ahmad and Akira Ogawa (Tokyo: The Okazaki Institute, 2001).

[2]   Stanley Weeks, "Military Responses to Transnational Security Threats". Paper presented to *Conference on Transnational Security Threats in Asia,* Asia-Pacific Center for Security Studies, Honolulu, 8–10 August 2000.

[3]   Hence the term "sea robbery", since piracy defined in international law occurs outside territorial waters, although the IMB's Regional Piracy Center and others include "sea robbery" in these figures and their own practical definition of piracy.

[4]   Robert Go, "Terrorism and Maritime Piracy Spur Leaders to Pledge Security Framework", 8 October 2003.

[5]   *Straits Times Interactive,* "ASEAN Ministers Seek Stronger Security Links", 8 January 2004.

[6]   Goh Sui Noi, "China to Sign Amity Treaty with ASEAN", *Straits Times,* 27 September 2003.

[7]   *Antara,* "RI, Malaysia Agree to Patrol Sipadan-Ligatan Waters Jointly", 16 December 2003.

[8]   *BBC Monitoring Asia-Pacific-Political,* "Philippines, Malaysia Begin Border Patrol Naval Exercises", 30 September 2003.

[9]   See Mukundan, this volume, for substantiation of this point.

[10] Peter Alford, "Plague of Piracy in Trade Lane", *The Australian,* 3 February 2001.

[11] Mark Husband, "WMRC Report Blames Indonesian Corruption for Rise in Piracy in South-East Asian Waters", *The Financial Times,* 14 February 2004.

[12] John J. Brandon, "High-Seas Piracy is Booming: It's Time to Fight Harder", *The Christian Science Monitor,* 27 December 2000.

[13] *BBC Monitoring Asia-Pacific,* "Indonesian Navy Says Pirates Capitalizing on Regional Unrest", 1 April 2001.

[14] *Xinhua,* "Indonesian Navy to Send Warships to Aceh", 22 March 2001; ironically, the decrease in the number of piracy incidents in the Strait in May and June of 2003 was attributed to Indonesia's deployment of naval warships and troops to Aceh to suppress the GAM.

[15] Paul Wiseman, "Pirates Loot the Fruits of 21st Century Trade", *USA Today,* 1 February 2001.

[16] "New Seaborne Piracy Pact to be Signed by Asian Nations", *Asia Pulse,* 22 September, 2003.

[17] Anonymous, "Japan to Hold Anti-Piracy Drills with Malaysia, India", *Business Times Shipping Times,* 1 November 2000, <http://www.businesstimes. asial.com.sg>.

[18] Information from Japan Coast Guard.

[19] *Financial Times,* "Politics and Law: Vietnam, Japan Vow to Broaden Military Co-operation", 10 November 2003.

20 Donald Urquhart, "Japan to Hold Anti-Piracy Drills with Thailand", *Business News*, 26 February 2004.

21 Kyodo News Service, "Japan to Send Patrol Vessel to Singapore for Antipiracy", 19 November 2003.

22 *Business Times*, "Maritime Offenses Bill Passed", 11 November 2003; <http://www.imo.org/home.asp> Status of Conventions by country (October 2004).

23 *Gaimusho* (Ministry of Foreign Affairs), *Genjou no kaizoku mondai to Nihon Kouken, Gaimushou* homepage, December 2001 at <http://wwwmofa.go.jp>.

24 Donald Urquhart, "Japan Helping to Set Up Coast Guard: Indon Team was in Japan to Study Operations of Japan Coast Guard", *Business Times/Shipping Times*, 25 March 2003.

25 Mohamed Nazalina, "Coast Guard to Fight Sea Threats", *The Star online*, 16 April 2002.

26 Mark J. Valencia, "Navigating Neptune's Realm", *Confidence Building Measures and Security Issues in Northeast Asia*, edited by Benjamin L. Self and Yuki Tatsumi (Washington D.C., The Henry L. Stimson Center, February 2000), pp. 1–37.

27 Stanley Weeks, "Piracy in East Asia: Trends and Counter-measures". Paper presented to the *Eleventh Asia-Pacific Roundtable*, Institute for Strategic and International Studies, Kuala Lumpur, 5–8 June 1997.

28 Donald Urquhart, "UN-Backed Multi National Force Needed to Curb Piracy", *The Business Times*, 4 March 2004

29 Mark J. Valencia, "Joining Up with Japan to Patrol Asian Waters", *International Herald Tribune*, 28 April 2000, p. 6.

30 STRATFOR, "Japan Winning Hearts and Minds in Southeast Asia", 12 December 2003.

31 *The Honolulu Advertiser*, " Japan, Malaysia Engage in Pirate Drill", 19 November 2000, p. A-16.

32 Hidemichi Katsumoto, "View of Collective Self-Defense Right Draws Fire", *The Daily Yonuiri*, 30 November 2000.

33 *Asian Wall Street Journal*, "Pirates off Asia's Bow", 2 February 2001.

34 Arnold S. Tenorio, "With the US Security Proposal, Quo Vadis ARF?", *Businessworld (Philippines)*. 29 September 2000.

35 *Kyodo*, "Coastguard Officials from Japan, South Korea, Russia, USA meet in Tokyo", 20 December 2000.

36 Michael Richardson, "The Pirates Who Could Sink East Asia", *South China Morning Post*, 9 January 2004; Donald Urquhart, "Number, Violence of Piracy Attacks Increase", *Shipping Times*, 28 January 2004; Karl Malakunas, "Piracy Equals Terrorism on Southeast Asia's Troubled Waters", *Agence France Press*, 21 December 2003; *Honolulu Advertiser*, "Singapore Fears Ship-Bomb Attack", 14 November 2003, p. A10.

37 Michael Richardson, "Securing Choke Points at Sea Against Terrorists", *Straits Times*, 19 January 2004; Goh Chin Lan, "High-level Task Force to Boost Maritime Security", *Straits Times*, 3 March 2004; Donald Urquhart, "Task Force to Bolster Maritime Security", *Business Times*, 3 March 2004.

38 See also Valencia "Piracy and Terrorism", this volume.

39 *Asia Pulse*, "Manila Identified as Prone to Piracy Attacks," 9 September 2003.

40 International Chamber of Commerce, "New Brand of Piracy Threatens Oil Tankers in Malacca Strait", 2 September 2003.

41 *Philippine Daily Inquirer*, 3 September 2003.

42 *The Yomiuri Shimbun*, "Is Terrorism Heading for the High Seas", 7 October 2003.

43 Oliver Teves, "Ferry Blast Work of Islamic Rebels", *Honolulu Advertiser*, 29 February 2004, p. 1.

44 STRATFOR, "Washington and Jakarta: Sealing Security Seal", 21 October 2003.

45 *Indian Express*, "Marine Commando Unit to Fight Pirates in Andaman", 22 September 2003; *The Telegraph*, "US to Expand Scope of Military Exercises to Include Anti-Terror Measures", 30 September 2003.

46 Donald Urquhart, "Pirate Attacks will Lead to Disaster in Malacca Strait", *Shipping Times*, 29 October 2003; Donald Urquhart, "UN-Mandated Patrol of Malacca Strait Urged", 2 December 2003; Donald Urquhart, ASEAN Leaders Urged to Take Joint Action Against Piracy; *Business Times*, Singapore, 4 December 2003.

47 "An epistemic community is a broadly shared set of normative and principled beliefs, combined with an internalized and self-validating set of causal and methodological principles and a common policy goal operating within a set of formal, semiformal and informal institutions and networks that, in a period of dramatic historical change and uncertainty, provide the framework within which to broker a set of policy options drawn from their normative beliefs and amenable to their causal and explanatory principles." Michel Foucault may have invented the term "epistemic community" in *The Order of Things*, New York: Random House, 1970. However, as Ernst Haas has argued, Foucault's usage is indistinguishable from what might be called "ideological communities". For the meaning, definition, role, value, and examples of who may or may not constitute an epistemic community, see Burkhart Holzner and John H. Marx, *Knowledge Application*, Boston: Allyn and Baron, Inc., 1979, p. 108; Ernst Haas, *When Knowledge is Power*, Berkeley: University of California Press, 1990, pp. 40–46; The term epistemic community was first applied to international relations by John G. Ruggie, "International responses to technology, concepts and trends", *International Organization*, 29, no. 3 (Summer 1975): 569–70. See also Peter M. Haas, "Do regimes matter? epistemic communities and Mediterranean pollution control", *International Organization* 43, no. 3 (Summer 1989): 377–403. Much of

this section is excerpted from Weeks, "Military Responses to Transnational Security Threats", op. cit.

[48] The Guidelines for Regional Maritime Co-operation are available on the AUS.CSCAP website at <http://coombs.anu.edu.au/Depts/RSPAS/AUSSCAP/Guidelin.mcw.html>.

[49] Sam Bateman, personal communication, December 2004.

6

Piracy in Asia: International Co-operation and Japan's Role

Greg Chaikin[1]

Introduction

The demise of Soviet communism precipitated an "end of history" euphoria and heralded a new order in international affairs. This initial optimism eroded as Cold War configurations unravelled, revealing a complex interdependent world riddled with chronic turbulence. Where traditional security threats were conventional, inter-state fixated and visible, contemporary threats are unconventional, transnational and invisible. Low intensity security threats, such as insurgency, terrorism, piracy, transnational crime, people smuggling, and environmental degradation, are generally viewed as a by-product of intrastate conflict in the developing world.[2]

For many states in East Asia, the process of state building is unfinished business and globalization has only made this problem worse. Low intensity contingencies flourish under conditions of "rapid social and economic change undermining efforts to construct stable and legitimate governments and honest and effective systems of public administration and finance whilst maintaining an often fragmented national unity."[3]

Cold (- post cold) War militaries combating low intensity conflicts and transnational threats experience victorless campaigns and sullied reputations, detracting from their primary role as war-fighters.[4] There are constitutional and political limits on military involvement in internal security matters and traditional law enforcement. There is also the vexed problem of duplicitous and corrupt military sponsorship of piracy and arms smuggling to insurgents and secessionists.[5] Given these problems, it is worthwhile to consider the efficacy of bolstering civilian enforcement agencies and developing institutional building programmes, as they have the potential to achieve more effective and palatable outcomes.[6]

This chapter examines one example of low intensity conflict, namely maritime piracy.[7] It analyses regional policy responses to the piracy phenomenon and evaluates Japan's role in the emerging anti-piracy regime. It asserts that Japan, with its Peace Constitution, global economic reach, ODA power status and maritime history is ideally positioned to meet this challenge and fulfil Yoichi Funabashi's vision of Japan as a "global civilian power".[8] The chapter further asserts that as the majority of piratical attacks occur in territorial waters in East Asia,[9] law enforcement agencies are more likely to be the facilitators of regional maritime co-operation in the fight against piracy.

International Relations and the Maritime Realm

For much of the twentieth century, international relations scholarship has largely neglected the maritime realm. It has been the domain of international lawyers, maritime transport specialists, oceanographers, marine scientists, and environmentalists. Maritime issues were viewed as "soft politics" in the minds of "hard-minded terrestrials", playing a minor supporting role in international order matters.[10] One factor which may account for this oversight, is the conceptualization of the seas as an endless, inexhaustible, unpolluted, and unoccupiable space. These characteristics are embodied in Grotius' *mare librum*.[11] If the seas could not be inhabited and developed, states were unlikely to pursue their conquest, a key prerogative of sovereigns in the colonial era.

Another factor is the manner in which private maritime interests utilized the freedom of the seas concept. The freedom of the seas is an integral component of an open trading system. This was made possible by hegemonic sponsorship and the internationalization of the maritime transport sector in the mid-nineteenth century. It produced "an international regime comprised of a hybrid of public and private authorities".[12] Based on the freedom of the seas principle, a private international shipping regime evolved, placing regulatory control over ships, crew, cargo and transport in the hands of industry with little or no government involvement.[13]

Contemporary developments suggest that Grotian ideas are anachronistic and dangerous to global welfare and environmental order. For example, the rapid expansion of the international trading system, the depletion of fisheries, the sophistication of and demand for resource extraction technologies, and "creeping" state jurisdiction have made the maritime environment increasingly conflictual. Thus there is a trend towards increased regulation of the seas. For example, the 1982 United Nations Convention on the Law of the Sea (1982 UNCLOS), which came into effect in 1994, provides for the resolution of many maritime disputes through arbitration at the International Tribunal of the Law of the Sea. This has particular relevance to the seas of East Asia which are dominated by overlapping boundaries and an undeclared maritime arms build-up.[14]

International Regimes and Piracy

"International regimes" has emerged as a significant theoretical tool to explain rule-based co-operation in an anarchical international system. In essence, regimes are "specialized arrangements that pertain to well defined activities, resources, or geographical areas and often involve only some subset of the members of international society. Thus we speak of the international regimes for whaling ...." and potentially a regime for piracy repression.[15] The maritime realm is an ideal environment for regime construction as the high seas represent the archetypal notion of anarchy, where no higher authority exists. Even a hegemon may find small unconventional threats in a maritime context near impossible to defeat without some international co-operative mechanism in place.

One of the most significant international regimes is the 1982 UNCLOS which enjoys near universal acceptance save for the United States and a very few others. Its primary objectives are to manage ocean uses and resources. A key principle of ocean usage is the freedom of the high seas which is "not a self-contained legal principle, but is ancillary to and dependent upon another norm — the right to commerce and communication".[16] Therefore any damage to international shipping, intentional or otherwise, is an infringement of this norm, which is a key part of the infrastructure of the modern capitalist system.

Piracy is an impediment to the right to commerce and communication and Article 100 of the 1982 UNCLOS calls on all states to "co-operate to the fullest extent in the repression of piracy on the high seas or in any other place outside the jurisdiction of any State."[17] There has been a consistent recognition by states of the piracy problem and of the duty to repress it under international customary law (see Table 6.1). There are, however, no clear guidelines as to what constitutes co-operation to the "fullest extent."

Characterizing Piracy

Piracy has been described by international lawyers as *pirata este hostes generis* (an enemy of all mankind). Cinematically, pirates have been eulogised as romantic and rebellious figures resisting imperial tyranny

TABLE 6.1
International Convention Articles Regarding Piracy[18]

	UNCLOS 1982	Convention on the High Seas 1958	Harvard Agreement 1932
State duty to repress piracy	100	14	18
Definition of piracy	101	15	36
Naval/government vessels engaged in piracy	102	16	
Pirate ships defined	103	17	4
Nationally of pirate ships	104	18	5
Seizure of pirate ship	105	19	2, 13, 14, 15
Liability for unlawful seizure	106	20	10
Right to seizure	107	21	12
Right to ship visit	110	22	11
Right of hot pursuit	111	23	7, 8, 9

Source: See footnote 18.

and seeking egalitarian freedom. Contemporary commentators rebuke these Hollywood images as false, as pirates were and are brutal and greedy thugs. Modern pirates may even take on the mantle of "terrorists". This is a broader conception of piracy than scholars have pursued to date. Nevertheless, pirates are multidimensional, as their seafarer skills can be applied to other criminal genres, such as people smuggling, arms dealing, drug trafficking and "fish piracy".[19]

Underlying Causes of Piracy's Persistence

There are five characteristics of piracy: human character; geography; economics; state-pirate interactions; and ideas and actions of political communities.[20] There are three points worth reiterating. First, where the economic costs of piracy are minimal in relation to the costs of suppression, budget allocations and policy directives for effective policing are unlikely to be forthcoming. This is especially true where maritime forces are prioritized for activities severely impacting state integrity, such as Indonesian military actions against secessionists in Aceh.[21]

Second, piracy flourishes when states are unconsolidated and sovereign authority over land is yet incomplete. Imposition of authority over the sea is a difficult task for the state to achieve and often requires international support to effectively suppress piracy.[22]

Third, as territorial order is a major concern for sovereign states, periods of warfare, political turmoil and economic downturn provide opportunities for the less scrupulous and poverty-stricken to take advantage of state weakness and diminished capacity to provide human security.[23]

This parallels the situation in many East Asian states, especially Indonesia and the Philippines, where piracy and terrorism are problematic. Since the Asian financial crisis, fragmentary pressures exacerbated by poverty and dissatisfaction with fiscal redistribution have provided fertile ground for violent political resistance and crime.[24]

Is Piracy a Serious Threat to Regional Security?

Sea-lane Security

Geostrategically, the Malacca/Singapore Straits and the South China Sea are two of the world's busiest sea-lanes and straddle one of the world's most important inter-ocean basins. It is estimated that 41,000 ships or vessels pass through these sea-lanes every year. This highlights the heavy dependence of East Asia's economies on sea-borne trade.[25]

Intraregional and interregional trade has been central to the rise in East Asia's economic fortunes. Sea-lane usage will increase in line with expected national growth patterns of the major Northeast Asian economies. Activities such as piracy could impact the free passage of trade and potentially undermine the economic welfare of littoral states as well as disrupt the smooth delivery of key energy resources and international trade.

Territorial Security

In addition to sea-lane security, a key element of East Asian security is "fixated on issues of territorial integrity." "For most countries in the region increasing self-reliance against regional contingencies involves a primary emphasis on defence of the maritime approaches." One only needs to look at the furore over Chinese actions in the South China Sea or the Daiyou/Senkaku islands dispute to recognize the simmering volatility of issues relating to maritime boundaries and offshore territorial claims. In fact, maritime boundary disputes and offshore territorial claims, account for a third of all potential regional conflicts.[26] This situation has been exacerbated in East Asia with the entry into force of the 1982 UNCLOS in 1994. Regional states have turned their attention to claiming maritime territories and resource zones and this is reflected in naval budgets emphasizing the acquisition of offshore surveillance type vessels and aircraft.[27] In this context unimpeded piracy poses a threat to state security. It signals to neighbours weaknesses in state capacity to maintain sovereign integrity, and thus undermines maritime territorial and jurisdictional claims.

Environmental Issues

There is also the distinct possibility of piratical acts leading to a major environmental accident. There are International Maritime Bureau (IMB) reports of ships underway being attacked and left without anyone in command enhancing the possibility, particularly in narrow sea-lanes, for such vessels to run aground. Should a fully laden oil tanker be sunk, the consequences for coastal communities and the fishing industry would be environmentally disastrous, not to mention the effects on navigation.[28]

Counter-Piracy Efforts in East Asia

The outbreak of piracy attacks in the Straits of Malacca/Singapore, the Phillip Channel and the South China Seas in the early 1990s led Indonesia, Malaysia, Singapore, and the Philippines to institute a number of counter piracy initiatives. These included improved information exchange and co-operation between law enforcement agencies and the co-ordination of surveillance patrols by maritime police and naval forces.

In addition, a number of bilateral agreements were implemented such as the Indo-Sin Co-ordinated Patrols (ISCP)[29] and the Malaysia-Philippines Memorandum of Understanding. Malaysia and Indonesia also reactivated a joint naval exercise, Malindo Jaya. Although these arrangements initially proved effective in substantially reducing piracy attacks, eradication was not achieved.[30]

Piracy returned with greater virulence in the wake of the 1997 Asian crisis. The economic and political fallout led to a breakdown of law and order in Indonesia and elsewhere. The severe reduction in defence spending across East Asia reduced the effectiveness of maritime co-operative arrangements. And military personnel and military supported militia were widely suspected of participating in piracy.[31]

Association of Southeast Asian Nations (ASEAN)

ASEAN actively supported bilateral responses to piracy but has refrained from undertaking a more robust multilateral response due to concerns that violations of traditional concepts of sovereignty may occur. To combat transnational crime, ASEAN developed a number of initiatives through institutional bodies such as the ASEAN Ministerial Meeting on Transnational Crime, the ASEAN Finance Ministers Meeting (AFMM), the ASEAN Chiefs of National Police (ASEANAPOL), and the ASEAN Senior Officials on Drugs Matters (ASOD).

At the inaugural meeting of the ASEAN Ministers of Interior/Home Affairs on 20 December 1997, the ASEAN Declaration on Transnational Crime sought to develop approaches to fight transnational crime through regional collaboration and international co-operation. Supporting this initiative was the establishment of the ASEAN Ministerial Meeting on Transnational Crime (AMMTC). In June 1999 AMMTC adopted the ASEAN Plan of Action (POA) to combat transnational crime.

The POA involves bolstering ASEAN member countries' efforts to combat transnational crime from the national and bilateral levels to the regional dimension and strengthening regional commitments. The Plan includes information exchange, co-operation in legal and law enforcement matters, institutional capacity building, training and extraregional co-operation.

Another key development is the establishment of the ASEAN Centre for Combating Transnational Crime (ACTC), which promotes data resource sharing and assists in the implementation of programme activities outlined in the proposed action plan. ACTC is also a repository of information on national legislation, regulatory measures and jurisprudence of individual member countries.[32]

At the May 2002 ASEAN Senior Officials Meeting (SOM), uniform laws in relation to transnational crime were discussed including piracy and terrorism. Harmonization of national laws on transnational crime was viewed as a matter of high priority. The advantage of uniform laws is that it leads to greater certainty in international co-operation with a greater likelihood of successful prosecutions. As Malaysian Deputy Home Affairs Minister Chor Chee Heiung stated "when a criminal act takes place in different jurisdictions successful prosecution relies upon effective regional and international co-operation" and the implementation of extradition and mutual assistance treaties.[33] Malaysia has usually been the most vocal opponent of external interference and initially resisted Japan's anti-piracy initiatives. Thus this is a major step forward for ASEAN. Although piracy was not the impetus for this policy shift, it sets a new benchmark for permissible intervention.

ASEAN Regional Forum (ARF)

The ASEAN Regional Forum adopted the ASEAN way, emphasizing the process "of building a dense web of relations between member countries," through confidence building measures (CBMs), preventative diplomacy, and developing approaches to conflict. Co-operative security rather than collective defence reflects ARF's *modus operandi*: "habits of dialogue" facilitate confidence building with the potential for the peaceful resolution of disputes.

In November 1999 piracy issues were discussed at an ARF Maritime Senior Officials Meeting held in Honolulu. Recommendations included encouraging members to ratify maritime conventions and implement anti-piracy measures. In October 2000, the ARF established the Expert's Group Meeting on Transnational Crime initially focusing on piracy, illegal immigration and small arms.[34]

Beyond dialogue, CBMs, and *ad hoc* bilateral arrangements, more concrete co-operative regional security measures have not been forthcoming. ASEAN and ARF adherence to the principle of non-intervention is still a main impediment to well co-ordinated regional responses to maritime conflicts. This was illustrated by the reluctance of ASEAN to collectively address the Asian financial and East Timor crises.

Unlike Europe, the maritime geography of East Asia problematises the resolution of jurisdictional conflicts. Sovereign jurisdiction is a keenly and at times violently contested issue. Nevertheless given the exigencies of economic crisis, political instability and environmental degradation, there have been growing calls for the modification of the non-intervention principle including "constructive intervention" and "flexible engagement."[35]

Asia-Pacific Economic Co-operation (APEC)

Through its Transportation Working Group (TWG), APEC established the Experts Group on Maritime Safety. In 1997, the TWG tabled a study which identified safety issues and problems in the region including:

1. the completion of an interactive web-based Port Data Base;
2. the endorsement by the TPT-WG of the Mission Statement for the Maritime Initiative as a first step in promoting an efficient, safe and competitive operating environment for maritime transport in the region;
3. the completion of an inventory of existing regional co-operation arrangements with respect to oil spill preparedness and response;
4. the Joint Policy Statement on Satellite Navigation and Communications Systems establishing various co-operative actions to facilitate the implementation of satellite-based navigation and communications systems in the region, and the establishment of an advisory Committee to monitor actions; and
5. the Marine Resource Conservation Working Group.[36]

The Port Data Base and the satellite-based navigation systems provide important mechanisms to combat piracy. Also at the APEC meeting in Miyazaki, the inaugural Transportation Security Experts Group (TPT-SEG) recommended co-ordinating with the Maritime Safety Experts Group to address Asia-Pacific piracy.[37]

Council for Security Co-operation in the Asia-Pacific (CSCAP)

The Council for Security Co-operation in the Asia-Pacific (CSCAP) has a number of working groups two of which, Maritime Co-operation and Transnational Crime, have been active in proposing policy-oriented studies for Track One organizations. The Maritime Co-operation Group (CSCAP-MCG) has been meeting regularly each year since 1995. The CSCAP-MCG mandate includes maritime safety issues, resources conservation, oceans governance and unlawful activities at sea. In the 1998 Guidelines for Regime Maritime Co-operation, a set of basic binding principles were developed regarding the co-ordination of maritime enforcement activities.

After a joint meeting with the CSCAP Working Group on Transnational Crime in November 1999, the CSCAP Maritime Co-operation Working Group at its November 2000 Beijing meetings agreed to a more detailed CSCAP Memorandum on Co-operation for Law and Order at Sea. It also recommended harmonizing piracy laws/jurisdiction, identified the 1982 UNCLOS EEZ rights, and advocated anti-piracy agreements and information exchange.[38]

The Interests and Role of Japan

Japan as a Maritime Power

Since the Meiji era at the end of the nineteenth century, Japan's Navy and merchant fleet have been integral to the development of the modern Japanese state and its economic superpower status. Japan's Navy was the first in Asia to defeat a major European power in the Russo-Japanese War of 1905. This event marks a key foundation of Japanese nationalism and its imperialist adventures.

The Japanese Navy was viewed as a fundamental pillar of the state in protecting its Sea Lines of Communication (SLOC), securing access to energy sources and raw materials, and delivering its industrial exports. Ostensibly, the threat to Japan's SLOC security was the political and economic rationale for Japan's decision to wage war against the United States.

Since the end of the Second World War, Japan has been prohibited from developing offensive military forces. Article 9 of Japan's Constitution states:

> "Aspiring sincerely to an international peace based on justice and order, the Japanese people forever renounce war as a sovereign right of the nation and the threat or use of force as means of settling international disputes. In order to accomplish the aim of the preceding paragraph, land, sea, and air forces, as well as other war potential, will never be maintained. The right of belligerency of the state will not be recognized."[39]

Japan, like most other countries, has a foreign policy with the primary objective of promoting economic growth and prosperity and ensuring the security of its sovereign territory. Where Japan differs from other nation states is that it has for nearly fifty years adopted an "imbalanced" approach to foreign policy making. Throughout the Cold War, Japan steadfastly pursued the Yoshida Doctrine, combining a vigorous foreign economic policy while maintaining a junior partnership with the United States in politico-security affairs. Throughout the Cold War, Japan could maintain a low risk, low cost, and non-offensive posture supporting US foreign policy under the defence umbrella of the United States. However, this posture has come under increasing pressure as the *raison d'etre* of Cold War relationships disappeared.

After the First Iraq War in 1991, Japan shed its *happou bijn*[40] stance to security and embarked on a more proactive and assertive profile in international security issues. This process has gathered considerable momentum since September 11, 2001.

Indicators of Japan's changing security agenda include:

1. the dispatch of Maritime Self Defence Forces to the Indian Ocean in support of US forces in 2002; this was the first time Japanese forces participated in an ongoing military campaign since World War Two;
2. Japan launched two spy satellites in 2003, demonstrating an increasing desire to collect intelligence independently from its close ally, the United States;

3. the 2002 defence budget rose to 4,955 billion yen (US$42.5 billion) including an order for an advanced Aegis air system at a cost of 147 billion yen (US$1.14 billion);
4. Japan has plans to produce a PAC-3 (Patriot Advanced Capability) missile defence system with the United States;
5. there is speculation that the Japan Defence Agency (JDA) will be upgraded to full ministry status;[41] and
6. the recent passing of legislation on war contingencies expands the participatory role of the Japan's Self-Defence Forces (SDF) in military actions outside the country. The legislation allows Japanese forces to operate not only in times of war but also in response to terrorist incidents, kidnapping, abduction, and all other situations that threaten the lives of Japanese nationals and property.[42]

These developments have taken place despite constitutional constraints, political filibustering, and deep societal disapproval of militaristic tendencies. Japan now has the third largest military budget (US$42 billion 2002) after America and Russia. Its navy, the Maritime Self -Defence Force (MSDF) is the third largest navy in the world and possesses four Aegis, the US Navy's most sophisticated destroyers (See Table 6.2).[43]

Japan Coast Guard

The Japan Coast Guard (JCG) is administratively part of the Ministry of Land, Infrastructure and Transport and was known as the Japan Maritime

TABLE 6.2
Japan Maritime Self Defence Forces Profile (MSDF), 2000[44]

Active Personnel	42,700
Major Units	
Destroyer Flotillas	4
Destroyer Divisions	7
Submarine Divisions	6
Minesweeping Flotillas	1
Land based patrol Aircraft squadrons	13
Main Equipment	
Destroyers	50
Submarines	16
Combat aircraft	170

Source: See footnote 44.

Safety Agency until 2001. Its maritime hardware is formidable in regional terms and has an annual budget larger than most East Asian navies (see Table 6.3).

JCG is a well-managed organization with wide ranging experience in dealing with transnational maritime threats. JCG has acquired substantial institutional knowledge of the following issues: territorial disputes, for example the Northern Territories/Southern Kuriles, Senkaku/Daiyou and Takeshima/TokDo islands, people smuggling, fish pirates, drug smuggling, environmental pollution, mystery ships, and the notorious *ratchi mondai*. The *ratchi mondai* has created a great deal of media interest in Japan, especially after the North Korean government admitted kidnapping Japanese citizens, often from Japan's coastlines, during the 1970s and 1980s.[45]

Japan's Counter-Piracy Initiative

The key factors underpinning Japan's proactive policy in combating piracy in East Asia are:

1. Japan's dependence on sea borne trade and resources;
2. the opportunity to make a "physical" contribution to regional security;
3. the opportunity to enhance Japan's regional image and prestige; and
4. it supports Japanese claims for permanent seat status on the United Nations Security Council.

Although Japan's private maritime sector from the 1980s had initiated a number of ship security measures, policymakers did not take notice of piratical attacks against Japanese shipping interests until the early 1990s

TABLE 6.3
Japan Coast Guard Profile[46]

Active Personnel	12,700
Vessels	521
Aircraft	75

Source: See footnote 46.

(see Table 6.4). In 1993 Japan had informal talks with China in relation to pirate attacks in the East China Sea. In 1995 the Japan Defence Agency (JDA) published the National Defence Programme Outline (NDPO) which sought an increased military role for the Self Defence Forces in responding to unconventional security threats such as natural disasters, terrorism, and maritime piracy.[47]

Japan was galvanized into taking more robust action following a number of high profile sea-jackings affecting Japanese shipping interests (for example, the Petro Ranger, Tenyu, and Alondra Rainbow incidents). In 1999 the Nippon Foundation lobbied the Japanese Government to implement measures against piracy.[49] Former Prime Minister Obuchi broached the issue at the 1999 ASEAN leaders summit. He suggested the development of joint patrols by the region's national coast guards, enhanced information exchange, and an offer of financial assistance. This counter-piracy policy is commonly known as the Obuchi Initiative.[50]

The Obuchi Initiative was well received by most ASEAN countries.[51] The significance of the Obuchi Initiative was that Asian governments for the first time since the end of World War Two were considering a regional

TABLE 6.4
Reported Piracy Attacks Against Japanese Shipping, 1989–2002[48]

	East Asia	SE Asia	Indian Ocean	Africa	Americas	Other
1989	0	1				
1990	0	4				
1991	0	8				
1992	0	7				
1993	1	0		1		
1994	0	6	1		1	
1995	3	2	1		2	
1996	2	8		1		
1997	0	12	1	2		3
1998	0	14	1	4		
1999	1	27	6	1	1	3
2000	0	22	5		3	1
2001	0	4	3		3	
2002	0	12		2	1	1
Total	7	127	18	11	11	8

Source: See footnote 48.

security role for Japan. Tokyo contributed to the joint patrols by exclusively relying on its civilian controlled Japan Coast Guard rather than the Maritime Self Defence Forces (MSDF).[52] This ameliorated most regional concerns of a resurgent militaristic Japan.

In April 2000, the Regional Conference on Combating Piracy and Armed Robbery against Ships was held in Tokyo. It was sponsored by the Ministry of Foreign Affairs, the Ministry of Land Infrastructure and Transport, and the Nippon Foundation. Coast Guard chiefs and representatives of maritime organizations from fifteen countries were represented including Brunei, Cambodia, China, Hong Kong, India, Indonesia, Japan, Laos, Malaysia, Myanmar, Philippines, Republic of Korea, Singapore Thailand, and Vietnam. The conference participants agreed to a non-binding resolution pledging to step up co-operation against piracy and armed robbery on the high seas. The areas of co-operation include:

1. enhancement of law enforcement activities;
2. improved reporting procedures;
3. bilateral or multilateral assistance in investigation;
4. technical co-operation;
5. procedures for interception and seizure; and
6. information exchange.[53]

In November 2000, Japan held joint patrols with India and Malaysia.[54] In 2001 a JCG vessel visited Singapore, the Philippines, and Thailand and JCG aircraft were sent to Thailand and the Philippines as part of its anti-piracy programme. In 2002 JCG patrol vessels visited Indonesia, Brunei, India, and Singapore, and aircraft were sent to Brunei, Indonesia, the Philippines, Vietnam, Malaysia, and Singapore.[55] Despite recognition of Japan's interests, not to mention Japan's substantial financial contribution to the region's maritime safety and anti-piracy efforts, China refused to participate in joint maritime patrols with neighbouring states.[56]

A series of Expert Meetings on Piracy and Armed Robbery were held in Bangkok (2001), Kuala Lumpur (2002) and Manila (2003), supported by the Nippon Foundation. These meetings evaluated joint patrol exercises and assisted in the development of equipment and materials, as well as improved information networks.

The Ministry of Foreign Affairs (MOFA) is a significant broker in developing Japan's counter-piracy efforts. MOFA's policies to promote co-operation amongst Asian countries in the battle against piracy are:

1. to examine and follow-up regional co-operation agreements on antipiracy measures;
2. to raise the profile of the piracy problem at international meetings such as ASEAN+3 and encourage regional countries to become signatories to the Rome Convention as Singapore has recently done;
3. to support poverty counter-measures in areas where piratical attacks occur frequently;
4. to support the development of coast guard agencies, focusing on human resources development and technical assistance; and
5. to support ship industry activities that promote ship and port security.[57]

Japan's counter-piracy initiatives have had some successes. The Indonesian government has sought Japanese technical and financial assistance in creating a coast guard. And in March 2003 senior officials from the Indonesian Ministry of National Development Planning (BAPPENAS), the Marine and Air Police (POLAIRUD) and the Directorate General of Sea Communications (DGSC) visited Japan to study JCG operations.

The Indonesian Marine and Air Police and the Directorate General of Sea Communications will be merged into a newly established Indonesian Coast Guard (ICG). If the ICG becomes a reality, a number of countries, including the United States, have offered vessels and financial assistance.[58] Malaysia is also considering the consolidation of its 11 maritime law enforcement agencies into a Malaysian Coast Guard and the Japan Coast Guard has been mooted as the desired model.[59]

These developments suggest a shift from confidence building measures to increasing levels of co-operation and more vigorous individual state action to fight maritime piracy. As the Philippine Coast Guard Chief, Captain Wilfredo Tamayo noted at a recent Expert Meetings on Piracy and Armed Robbery in Manila:

> Such co-operation is the only solution when piracy transcends borders, when piracy comes hand in hand with economic, political and environmental issues and when piracy blends with other transnational crimes, foremost of which is maritime terrorism.[60]

Japan is undoubtedly a major maritime power in the region and is well equipped to take a leadership role in regional maritime affairs. The significance of Japan's contributions to the evolving piracy regime should not be underestimated. Japan has long desired to play a regional security role commensurate with its economic power and combating piracy is the beginning of a broader framework to safeguard its strategic and economic interests both regionally and beyond. The key to this policy is the use of a civilian maritime enforcement agency, rather than the military. Even though there has been some resistance to Japan's proposals, they appear to be both strategically and regionally palatable.

Notes

[1]   The author would like to thank the Mare Centre and the International Institute of Asian Studies for the invitation to present this paper and the provision of assistance to attend the People and the Sea II Conference, Amsterdam, The Netherlands, 4–6 September 2003.

Special thanks to Mark Beeson, Sam Bateman, Bill Tow and David Chaikin for their comments and support. The usual caveats apply and errors are solely that of the author.

[2]   Mohamed Ayoob, *The Third World Predicament: State Making, Regional Conflict and the International System* (Boulder: Lynne Rienner Publishers, 1995), Chapter 1.

[3]   T. Ertman, *Birth of the Leviathian: Building States and Regimes in Medieval and Early Modern Europe* (Cambridge: Cambridge University Press, 1997), p. 1.

[4]   J. Rosenau, *Along the Domestic-Foreign Frontier* (Washington D.C.: George Washington University Press, 1997), Chapter 19.

[5]   G. Teitler, "Piracy in South East Asia: A Historical Comparison", *MAST* no. 1 (2002): p. 77; D. Keene, "The Economic Functions of Violence in Civil Wars", *Adelphi Paper 320* (1997).

[6]   J. Rosenau, op. cit., Chapter 19.

[7]   A. Jordan, A. Amos, and W. Taylor, *American National Security* (Washington DC: John Hopkins University Press, 1999, 5th ed.), p. 238.

[8]   Y. Funabashi, "Introduction to Japan's International Agenda", in *Japan's International Agenda*, edited by Yoichi Funabashi (New York: New York University Press, 1994).

[9]   International Maritime Bureau Piracy Reports 1991 to 2002.

[10] The author acknowledges the tradition of Mahan and others who wrote of the significance of naval power to maritime strategy, but asserts that contemporary scholarship has given insufficient attention as non-military maritime issues become more pressing.

[11] P. Steinberg, *The Social Construction of the Oceans* (Cambridge: Cambridge University Press, 2002), Chapter 1.

[12] A. Claire-Cutler, V. Haufler, and T. Porter, *Private Authority and International Affairs* (New York: State University Press of New York, 1999), p. 283.

[13] The attitude of the shipping industry resistance to the establishment of the International Maritime Organization is a case in point.

[14] Sam Bateman, "Economic Growth, Marine Resources and Naval Arms in Asia: A Deadly Triangle", *Marine Policy* 22, no. 3 (1998): 78–112.

[15] Oran Young, *International Cooperation: Building Regimes for Natural Resources and the Environment* (New York: Cornell University Press, 1989), p. 235. See also special edition on international regimes in *International Organization* (1982) and Andreas Hasenclever, Peter Mayer, Volker Rittberger, *Theories of International Regimes* (Cambridge: Cambridge University Press, 1997).

[16] R. Lapidoth, "Freedom of Navigation — It's Legal History and its Normative Basis", *Journal of Maritime Law and Commerce*, no. 6 (1974–75): 263–71.

[17] United Nations, The Law of the Sea Official Text of the United Nations Convention on the Law of the Sea with Annnexes and Index (New York: St. Martin's Press, 1983,) p. 34.

[18] Adapted from K. Hayashi, *Kaiyouhou kenkyuu* [A Study of the Law of the Sea], (Tokyo: Nihon Hyouronsha, 1995), p. 103.

[19] C. Liss, "Maritime Piracy in Southeast Asia", *Contemporary Southeast Asian Studies* (2003): 63–64.

[20] J. Boulton, "Maritime Order and the Development of the International Law of Piracy", *International Relations* 11, no. 5 (1983): 2336–38.

[21] D. Urquhart, "Aceh Closure Wont Affect Malacca Straits Traffic: Insa; But US Navy Warns Shift in Resources May Lead to More Piracy Elsewhere", *Business Time/Shipping Times*, 16 June 2003.

[22] J. Boulton, op. cit., p. 2337.

[23] R. Thakur, "From National Security to Human Security", in *Asia-Pacific Security: The Economic-Politics Nexus*, edited by S. Harris and A. Mack (Canberra: Allen and Unwin, 1997), pp. 53–80.

[24] M. Beeson, "Globalization, Governance and the Political-Economy of the Public Policy Reform in East Asia", *Governance: An International Journal of Policy, Administration and Institutions* 14, no. 4 (2001): 481–502.

[25] Ji Guoxing, "SLOC Security in the Asia-Pacific", *Asia-Pacific Center for Security Studies* (*Occasional Paper 33*, February) (<http://www.apcss.org/Paper_SLOC_Occasional.htm>).

[26] Desmond Ball, "Arms and Affluence: Military Acquisitions in the Asia Pacific Region", *International Security* 18, no. 3 (Winter 1993–94): 82.

[27] J. McCaffrie, *Maritime Strategy into the Twenty-First Century: Issues for Regional*

Navies (Canberra: Strategic and Defense Studies, Australian National University, 1996), p. 11.

28 J. Abankyar, "Piracy and Ship Robbery: A Growing Menace" in *Combating Piracy and Ship Robbery*, edited by Hamzah Ahmad and Akira Ogawa (Tokyo: Okazaki Institute, 2001).

29 The Indo-Sin Co-ordinated Patrols (ISCP) are a combined sea-robbery patrol arrangement between the armed forces of Singapore and Indonesia. The arrangement calls for both parties to (1) exchange information on sea robberies; (2) establish effective lines of communication and facilities for hot pursuit; (3) patrol respective territorial waters during co-ordinated patrols; (4) abide by the guidelines for patrols pursuing offenders into territorial areas outside their jurisdiction.

30 Amitav Acharya, "A New Regional Order in Southeast Asia: ASEAN in the Post-Cold War Era", *Adelphi Paper 279* (1993), p. 70.

31 Interview with International Maritime Bureau official, 3 September 2001.

32 Various sites on the ASEAN secretariat homepage under Transnational Crime and International terrorism. See <http://www.aseansec.org>.

33 R. Ahmad, "Target: Cross-border crime PLAN: More Uniform Laws", *Straits Times*, 17 May 2002.

34 S. Pushpanathan, "Managing Transnational Crime in ASEAN". Paper presented to ASEAN Law Conference. ASEAN Secretariat, 1999, 1 July.

35 J. Furston, ASEAN and the Principle of Non-Intervention: Practice and Prospects sited at <http://www.iseas.edu.sg/trends520.pdf> (Singapore: Institute of Southeast Asian Studies, 2000), pp. 9–22.

36 Expert Group on Maritime Safety Report, APEC 17th Transportation Working Group Meeting, Singapore Shipping Association, 28 March 2000 <http://www.iot.gov.tw/apec_tptwg/TPT/tptmain/Steering-Committees/Safe/Experts-Group-on-Maritime-Safety/tptwg-17-final-papers/report-by-singapore.htm>.

37 Various pages at the APEC Secretariat, <http://www.apecsec.com>.

38 Desmond Ball, *The Council for Security in the Asia-Pacific (CSCAP): Its Record and its Prospects*. (Canberra: Strategic and Defense Studies Centre Australian National University, October 2000).

39 See Japan's constitution at <http://www.kantei.go.jp/foreign/constitution _and_government of_japan/constitution_e.html>.

40 *Happou bijin* is a common term used to describe Japan's "passive" foreign policy. A possible English translation would be "pollyanna-like" or "pretty from all directions".

41 The Japan Defense Agency relocated its main offices on 8 May 2000, to a 247.3 billion yen complex on the former site of the Japanese Imperial Army's Imperial

Headquarters in Ichigaya, near Shinjuku. At least 7,000 agency personnel with eight organizations were moved from the 40-year-old Minato-ku facility to the traditional Shinjuku-ku home of the military.

42 See Prime Minister's homepage for a translation of this legislation at <www.kantei.or.jp>.

43 International Institute of Strategic Affairs, *The Military Balance* (London: International Institute of Strategic Studies, 2001).

44 Source: <http://www.globalsecurity.org/military/world/japan/jmsdf.htm>.

45 Piracy information at *kaijou hoanchou* (Japan Coast Guard) <http://www.kaiho.or.jp>.

46 Japan Defense Agency, *The National Defense Programme Outline* (NDPO) at <http://www.jda.go.jp, http://www.jda.go.jp/e/policy/f_work/taikou/index_e.jtml>.

47 National Institute of Defense Studies, 1997: <http://www.iiss.org/confPress-more.php?confID=321>.

48 Adapted from the *Nippon Senshu Kyoukai* [Japan Shipping Association] Internet site: <http://www.jsanet.or.jp>.

49 The Nippon Foundation is a private philanthropic organization dedicated to maritime safety. More recently it has broadened its charitable agenda in education and health issues, both internationally and Japan. The Foundation's homepage has some English information but most piracy related information is in Japanese: <http://www.nipponfoundation.co.jp>.

50 D. Urquhart, "Obuchi to Urge ASEAN to Fight Piracy", *Business Times/Shipping Times* at <http://business-times.asia1.com.sg>, 22 November 1999; various articles from Nippon Foundation database.

51 S. Darmosumarto, "Japan offers counter-piracy programme", *Jakarta Post*, 4 April 2000. The Japan Maritime Safety Agency (MSA) changed its English name to the Japan Coast Guard (JCG) in 2001.

52 Japan Maritime Safety Agency (MSA) changed its English name to the Japan Coast Guard (JCG) in 2001.

53 *Nihon Senshu Kyoukai* [Japan Shipowner's Association] 2001 *Ajia kaizoku taisaku charenji 2000* [Japan's Anti-Piracy Challenge 2000] in *nihon senshu kyoukai,* homepage at <http://www.jsanet.or.jp>.

54 Anonymous, "Japan to Hold Anti-Piracy Drills with Malaysia, India", *Business Times/Shipping Times*, 1 November 2000 at <http://businesstimes.asia1.com.sg>.

55 Information received from JCG staff on 30 June 2003.

56 S. Darmosumarto, op. cit.

57 *Gaimusho* (Ministry of Foreign Affairs), *Genjou no kaizoku mondai to Nihon kouken, Gaimushou* homepage December 2001 at <http://www.mofa.go.jp>.

58   D. Urquhart, "Japan Helping to Set Up Coast Guard; Indon Team was in Japan
     to Study Operations of Japan Coast Guard", *Business Times/Shipping Times*,
     25 March 2003.
59   M. Nazlina, "Coast Guard to Fight Sea Threats", *The Star online*, 16 April 2003;
     D. Urquhart, "Malaysia Acts to Create National Coast Guard", *Business Times/
     Shipping Times*, 8 July 2003.
60   D. Urquhart, "Asian Nations Given Anti-Piracy Guidelines", *Business Times/
     Shipping Times*, 11 March 2003.

7

Combating Piracy:
Co-operation Needs, Efforts,
and Challenges

Hasjim Djalal

The 1982 UN Law of the Sea Convention
(UNCLOS) and Piracy

With regard to piracy itself, the 1982 UNCLOS Article 100 obliges "all states to co-operate to the fullest possible extent in the repression of piracy". Article 101 defines piracy as:

1. any illegal acts of violence or detention, or any act of depredation, committed for private ends by the crew or the passenger of a private ship or a private aircraft, and directed : (1) on the high seas, against another ship or aircraft, or against persons or property on board such ship or aircraft; (2) against a ship, aircraft, persons or property in a place outside the jurisdiction of any state;
2. any act of voluntary participation in the operation of a ship or of an aircraft with knowledge of facts making it a pirate ship or aircraft;

3. any act of inciting or of intentionally facilitating an act described
    in paragraph (a) or (b).

Thus piracy is an illegal act "on the high seas or in any other place outside
the jurisdiction of any state". An act of piracy which takes place in waters
under national jurisdiction, therefore, is not an act of piracy, but armed
robbery or sea robbery which must be dealt with exclusively by the state
under the principle of coastal state sovereignty and national security.

Given this definition and taking into account the 1982 UNCLOS Article
86, and without prejudice to the freedom of navigation and overflight in
the EEZ, it would appear that an act of piracy within the EEZ would also
be within national jurisdiction, since the high seas are generally understood
to be an area beyond the EEZ. The freedom of navigation is assured in the
EEZ by the 1982 UNCLOS Articles 58 paragraph 1 and Article 87 paragraph
1a. Because an armed robbery could interfere with the freedom of
navigation, it would appear that an act to prevent armed robbery in the
EEZ could be the subject of co-operation between states.

According to the 1982 UNCLOS Article 102, if the act of piracy is
committed by a warship or government ship controlled by a crew which
has mutinied, the warship or the government ship would be regarded as
a private ship which has committed piracy and therefore would be subjected
to the rules of piracy. And according to the 1982 UNCLOS Article 103, a
ship or aircraft would be considered a pirate ship or pirate aircraft if it is
dominated by persons who have the intention to use the ship to commit
an act of piracy. The ship may retain its nationality, although it has become
a pirate ship, depending upon the law of the state which has granted its
nationality in the first place. The pirates, and the property on board, may
be seized from a pirate ship on the high seas or any other place outside the
jurisdiction of any state. The penalties to be imposed as well as action to
be taken with regard to the seized pirate ship would be determined by the
court of the state which carries out the seizure (1982 UNCLOS Article 105).
However, if it can be proven that the seizure has been effected without
adequate grounds, the state(s) making the seizure shall be liable for any
loss or damage caused by it (1982 UNCLOS Article 106).

A seizure on account of piracy may be carried out only by a warship or
military aircraft, or other ship or aircraft clearly marked and identifiable
as being on government service and authorized to that effect (1982 UNCLOS
Article 107). It appears from this Article that a warship or military aircraft

is allowed to seize pirate ships on the high seas simply by the fact that they are a warship or military aircraft without a need for further authorization, while other ships or aircraft being on government service can only do so if they are authorized to do so by the flag state.

The Indonesian Situation

Indonesia is a large maritime and archipelagic state in the Asia Pacific region. It controls about 3 million km^2 of archipelagic waters and territorial sea, plus another 3 million km^2 of EEZ and continental shelf. It also controls several important sea-lanes between the Pacific and the Indian Oceans. While these extensive maritime zones offer enormous economic potential for the development of the country, they also bring with them the enormous tasks of protecting them as well as maintaining law and order at sea and the national unity of this archipelagic country.

Indonesia would need more than 300 vessels able to protect its maritime space and resources, as well as port facilities, human resources and technology dedicated to that purpose. But it has only about 115 vessels total for this purpose, and of these, only about 25 vessels that are operating at sea at any given time. The current political, economic and financial crisis in Indonesia has aggravated the problem of law enforcement at sea as well as that of maintaining maritime order and preventing the disintegration of the country. Consequently, there has been substantial slackening in law enforcement and security at sea; and this problem is more acute in Indonesia's EEZ.

The major problems for Indonesia at the moment are (a) to prevent armed robberies at sea and to promote co-operation with neighbouring countries to combat armed robbery and piracy, (b) to prevent illegal fishing by foreign vessels which are depleting Indonesian resources and depriving the Indonesian government of its legitimate income, (c) to protect and patrol Indonesian archipelagic sea-lanes which are so important for regional and global maritime trade and military strategy, especially in a time of regional and global crisis, and, (d) to prevent the use of Indonesian maritime zones for illegal acts at sea, including illicit traffic in drugs and arms, maritime terrorism, and illegal refugees transiting to third countries.

Indonesia does not have the enormous financial resources that would be required to protect its maritime zones. As an example, Singapore, a country of less than 700 km^2, spent US\$4.2 billion on its military in 1999 or roughly 24.9 per cent of its total government budget. Indonesia, a country of about 8,000,000 km² of land and sea, spent only US$1.5 billion in 1999, or roughly 5.9 per cent of its total government expenditure, or about 0.8 per cent of its GDP for defence purposes. Other countries, including those in the region, spent much more. For example, Japan spent 1.2 per cent of its GDP for defence purposes, Australia 1.8 per cent, Germany 1.5 per cent, France 2.4 per cent, the United Kingdom 2.5 per cent, and the United States 3.3 per cent (before the Iraq war). Thus Indonesian defence spending is still among the lowest in the region, in both dollar value and in relation to GDP.

Indonesia is fully aware that incidents of piracy and armed robbery have risen significantly in 2000 and 2002 in comparison with 1999. Indeed, most of the armed robberies in 2000–02 in Southeast Asia occurred in Indonesian waters, particularly in its archipelagic waters between Singapore and the Java Sea, in the Malacca Strait, and in the South China Sea. Within the first half of 2003 alone, out of 234 incidents worldwide, 64 took place in Indonesian waters, or more than 25 per cent of the total. These incidents included 43 ships boarded, 4 hijacked, and 17 attempted attacks against ships.

Indonesia also recognizes that although piracy and armed robbery are a scourge in themselves, they also endanger the safe navigation of ships and increase the danger of collision or grounding. This in turn endangers the marine environment, particularly when armed robbery or piracy involves large oil tankers. These dangers are multiplied in the Straits of Malacca and Singapore and the South China Sea where more than 600 ships transit each day.

Thus Indonesia is concerned and is trying to address the problem. With regard to the western waters, particularly the approach to Singapore through the Karimata Straits, there is already a plan to strengthen Indonesian law enforcement capabilities in the area, particularly by increasing surveillance and monitoring systems and response capabilities. But the study indicated that it would cost Indonesia about US$38.5 million for an anti piracy command and control centre between the Strait of Singapore and Jakarta. Unfortunately, Indonesia does not presently have sufficient funds for that purpose, and is actually accumulating billions of dollars in foreign debt.

With regard to the Straits of Malacca and Singapore, Indonesia, Malaysia, and Singapore have been co-operating to promote the safety of navigation with the support of Japan for the last twenty years. This co-operation has resulted in improved navigational aids and hydrographic charts as well as other safety measures. The three coastal states, through bilateral mechanisms, have also co-operated and co-ordinated their patrols to deal with illegal acts at sea, particularly armed robbery. Yet obviously more needs to be done to promote the safety of navigation, including the prevention of sea robbery and the protection of the marine environment in those waters. And with regard to the South China Sea, Indonesia, together with other littoral authorities, has taken the initiative to promote co-operation on safety of navigation, shipping and communication.

The 1982 UNCLOS Article 43 encourages co-operation between user states and states bordering a strait, (a) "in the establishment and maintenance of necessary navigational and safety aids or other improvements in aid of international navigation, and (b) for the prevention, reduction and control of pollution from ships". So far only Japan has co-operated with the three coastal states with regard to installing navigational aids, hydrographic surveys, and other means to promote safety of navigation in the Straits of Malacca and Singapore. Little or no co-operation or assistance has been forthcoming from the other user states to prevent, reduce, and control pollution from ships, or to help the coastal states, particularly Indonesia, combat piracy and armed robbery in the area, despite the fact that these measures could be regarded as "other improvements in aid of international navigation". In addition, although Article 43 deals with the promotion of safety of navigation and control of pollution in "straits used for international navigation", there is no reason that it could not to apply to archipelagic sea-lanes as well if the archipelagic state concerned requested it.

There is no doubt that Indonesia needs help to maintain law and order at sea and to protect its maritime resources and national unity. But Indonesia would not welcome maritime countries escorting their vessels with their coastguards or navies when they navigate Indonesian waters. Nor would Indonesia welcome commercial cargo vessels or tankers with armed guards navigating Indonesian waters. Indeed, the presence of foreign armed vessels or commercial vessels with armed guards could create more problems and complications rather than solutions. On the other hand, Indonesia would welcome an initiative from the user states as well as other stake holders to: (a) assist Indonesian law enforcement and security efforts at sea by maintaining and strengthening their capabilities through aid, equipment and training, and (b) help organize and co-ordinate co-operative efforts and linkages with regional or other interested parties.

In Indonesia there are many agencies involved in enforcement activities at sea, although they have been co-ordinated during the last few years by the *Bakorkamla*, a Co-ordinating Agency for Security at Sea, commanded by the Commander of the Armed Forces. Practice indicates, however, that it has not been easy to co-ordinate the activities of the various law enforcement agencies. Lately, there has been considerable discussion regarding the efficiency and effectiveness of *Bakorkamla*, particularly after the separation of the Police from the Armed Forces. A number of proposals have been made, such as the separation of the functions of maintaining "national security" (which should be the responsibility of the TNI — the Indonesian Armed Forces — and "law enforcement" at sea which should be the responsibility of the Police), with a proposal to delegate the latter function to the Coast Guard (although Indonesia has no Coast Guard as such). None of these proposals have yet been approved, and studies and discussions are continuing.

Regional Approaches

In Malaysia, there are seven agencies that are authorized to enforce various maritime legislation, namely the Royal Malaysian Police (Marine), the Fishery Department, the Royal Customs and Excise Department, the Marine Department, the Royal Malaysian Navy (RMN), the Department of Environment, and the Immigration Department. All these agencies, except the RMN, which only lends assistance to the others, are principal implementers of specific legislation and conduct their own operations in their own designated area of responsibility. However, the RMN and the Royal Malaysian Air Force are responsible for the conduct of operations and surveillance over the Malaysian EEZ while other agencies are responsible for the territorial sea. In 1985 Malaysia established a Maritime Enforcement Co-ordinating Centre (MECC) under the National Security Division of the Prime Minister's Department. The MECC monitors all maritime activities and compiles information for distribution to relevant maritime enforcement agencies. It does not, however, exercise any command or control function over any of the agencies.

There have been a number of armed robberies in the Gulf of Thailand and in the Andaman Sea, although the number is not as large as in other parts of Southeast Asia. The Royal Thai Navy, in addition to defending the country, also protects the country's maritime interests and aids other national agencies in implementing their respective areas of responsibility. The Royal Thai Navy has established a Coast Guard Command for the purpose of law enforcement and aiding people in its territorial sea and contiguous zone.

While each country in Southeast Asia is strengthening their own respective enforcement agencies, they have also been co-operating with each other. This co-operation includes the following arrangements.

1. The 1992 Indonesia-Singapore Agreement on co-ordination of patrols and hot pursuit to combat piracy and armed robbery at sea has been instrumental in reducing the incidence of armed robbery in the Strait of Singapore, at least until the advent of the economic crisis in Indonesia in 1998. Experience has indicated that for the Agreement to be more effective, there is a need to intensify police activities on land to target the pirates' bases.

2. There is a similar arrangement between Indonesia and Malaysia under the auspices of the General Border Committee (GBC) which was established in December 1992. The GBC also established an operational co-ordinating border arrangement (Maritime Operation Planning Team) to discuss and map-out strategies to deal with maritime issues arising along the common border. This arrangement has also enhanced bilateral co-operation between the two countries in combating illegal activities, including co-ordinated maritime patrol operations in the Strait of Malacca.

3. A Malaysia-Philippines Border Patrol Co-ordinating Group (MPBPCG) has also been established through which the enforcement agencies of Malaysia and the Philippines conduct co-ordinated border patrol operations in the maritime areas for the prevention of armed robbery and illegal activities at sea. Under the arrangement, all border patrol operations shall be in accordance with the laws and regulations of the respective countries and in conformity with international law. The co-ordinated/combined operations have been able to curb cross-border illegal activities and armed robbery between the two countries.

4. There has also been similar co-operation between Malaysia and Singapore in which the police departments of the two countries

share information and discuss maritime issues and criminal
activities affecting both countries

5. The Royal Thai Navy has also tried to build up good relations with
    its neighbours for the purpose of protecting their mutual interests
    at sea. The RTN and the RMN have conducted joint patrols along
    their sea boundaries, both in the Gulf of Thailand and in the
    Andaman Sea, to prevent arms trafficking and other illegal acts.
    Thailand has also reached a maritime boundary agreement with
    Vietnam, which has helped solve problems the two navies faced
    when the boundary was unresolved.

ASEAN Efforts

ASEAN itself has many initiatives attempting to combat piracy and
armed robbery in ASEAN seas. The ASEAN work programme to
implement the ASEAN Plan of Action to Combat Transnational Crimes
adopted in Kuala Lumpur on 17 May 2002, includes an agreement to
work together on sea piracy regarding information exchange, legal
matters, law enforcement, training, institutional and capacity building,
and extra-regional co-operation.

Specifically, the Agreement includes commitments to:

1. establish a compilation of national laws and regulations of ASEAN
    member countries pertaining to piracy and armed robbery at sea,
    which is to lead towards establishing a regional repository of such
    national laws and regulations to be made available on the
    ASEANWEB.
2. exchange of information and enhanced co-operation with the
    International Maritime Organization (IMO) as well as with other
    bodies involved in combating piracy and armed robbery at sea,
    such as the International Maritime Bureau (IMB), the Federation of
    ASEAN Shipowners Association (FASA), and ASEANAPOL.
3. compile national studies to determine trends and the "modus
    operandi" of piracy in Southeast Asian waters.
4. consider the feasibility of developing multilateral or bilateral legal
    arrangements to facilitate apprehension, investigation, hot pursuit,
    prosecution and extradition, exchange of witnesses, sharing of
    evidence, inquiry, seizure and forfeiture of the proceeds of the

crime in order to enhance mutual legal and administrative assistance among ASEAN Member Countries.

5. enhance co-ordinated anti-piracy patrols.
6. enhance co-operation and co-ordination in law enforcement and intelligence sharing of piracy and armed robbery at sea and that of other transnational crimes.
7. strengthen and enhance existing co-operation among National Focal Points of ASEAN Countries involved in combating and suppressing piracy and armed robbery at sea.
8. enhance and seek training programmes within ASEAN and with the ASEAN Dialogue Partners to equip maritime, customs, the police, port authority and other relevant officials for the prevention and suppression of sea piracy and other maritime crimes.
9. seek technical assistance from users of the waterways and relevant specialized agencies of the United Nations and other international organizations, particularly with regard to training and acquisition of effective communication equipment and assets; this would be in accordance with the 1982 UNCLOS Article 43.
10. obtain financial assistance for increased patrolling of particularly vulnerable sea areas and for training programmes for maritime law enforcement officials and the agencies concerned.

The South China Sea Workshop Process

There have been several attempts to promote co-operation on this matter within the region. A prime example is the Workshop on Managing Potential Conflicts in the South China Sea, which considered this matter at its first Workshop in Bali in 1990 within the context of promoting safety of navigation, shipping and communication in the South China Sea. In the Second Workshop in Bandung in July 1991, it was agreed that the areas of co-operation in the South China Sea "may include co-operation to promote safety of navigation and communication, to co-ordinate search and rescue, to combat piracy and armed robbery, to promote the national utilization of living resources, to protect and preserve the marine environment, to conduct marine scientific research, and to eliminate illicit traffic in drugs in the South China Sea". During the Third Workshop in Yogyakarta in 1992, it was decided that the problems of safety of navigation should be further discussed within a Technical Working Group on Safety of Navigation,

Shipping and Communication (TWG-SNSC) in order to study the problems more carefully so that the possibilities for co-operation in the various areas identified during the First and Second Workshops could be enhanced.

However due to several technical difficulties in organizing the meeting of the TWG-SNSC, the First TWG-SNSC was not held until October 1995, in Jakarta. Several topics were discussed at this meeting, including exchange of information and data on safety of navigation, shipping and communications, including improvements to radio beacon systems and weather information and networking; education and training programmes for mariners; development of contingency plans and a Search and Rescue (SAR) network; co-operation in hydrographic and oceanographic surveys; and co-operation to combat piracy, illicit drug trafficking and problems of refugees at sea.

Since 1995, the Workshops have agreed that:

1. co-operation on SNSC is desirable and possible despite unresolved territorial and jurisdictional issues;
2. the UNCLOS 1982 and IMO Conventions provide a useful framework and basis for efforts to deal with the complex navigational, shipping and communications issues in the South China Sea;
3. governments in the South China Sea region should accede to IMO Conventions and Agreements pertaining to SNSC;
4. South China Sea states should adopt the Tokyo Memorandum of Understanding on Port State Control in the Asia Pacific region;
5. priorities such as training and improving the competence of seafarers, the corresponding development of ships, regional facilities and implementation of information systems require further discussion;
6. it would be desirable to hold a specialized meeting of experts on training of mariners to discuss the points presented at the Workshop pertaining to co-operation and co-ordination in the training of seafarers among the South China Sea states and Workshop participants;
7. there is a need to enhance multilateral co-operation and co-ordination among SAR agencies in the South China Sea;
8. the relevant authorities would draw up a SAR Plan for the South China Sea taking into account the proposals made at the SAR Meeting in Tokyo in December 1986;

9. it would be useful to urge relevant authorities to delimit their respective areas of SAR responsibilities which in some cases overlap, with a view to enhancing the efficacy of co-ordinated and well-linked SAR operations in the South China Sea;

10. the authorities in the South China Sea should consider the possibility of establishing a regional ship reporting system and a ship transponder system in the interest of safety of navigation; and

11. enforcement officials of the South China Sea Workshop countries should discuss how to deal more effectively with piracy issues and whether and in what way the TWG-SNSC can facilitate such co-operative ventures.

12. The following participants were assigned the task of preparing initiatives or studies:
   - Singapore: Education and Training of Mariners
   - Malaysia: Unlawful Activities at Sea and SAR
   - Chinese-Taipei: Exchange of Hydrographic Data and Information
   - China: Contingency Plans for Pollution Control.

The results of the TWG-SNSC were reported to and discussed at the Sixth Workshop in Balikpapan in October 1995 which endorsed them and agreed to convene the Second TWG-SNSC to continue the work in this field. The Second TWG-SNSC was held in Bandar Seri Begawan in October 1996 and discussed the topics identified in the First TWG-SNSC, particularly the assignments identified above. On Unlawful Activities at Sea and SAR, the Second TWG-SNSC agreed that:

1. unilateral efforts should be continued and strengthened where both unlawful acts and SAR are concerned;

2. bilateral co-operation should also be continued and enhanced;

3. an Experts Meeting should be convened to address regional arrangements on both SAR and Unlawful Activities at Sea;

4. the possibility of holding a regional forum on SAR with the support of the appropriate authorities should be discussed;

5. the exchange of data and information on Unlawful Acts at Sea should be enhanced in the region and it was thought this could be done in co-operation with the IMB-RPC in Kuala Lumpur as the focal point for the collection of regional information; and

6. a meeting should be held to consider how to operationalize the following suggestions:

- SAR training exchanges;
- exchange of officers;
- exchange of SAR operating manuals;
- joint exercises;
- exchange of visits by SAR officials;
- development of multilateral or bilateral SAR Agreements; and
- accession to the 1979 SAR Convention.

The Third Meeting of the TWG-SNSC was held in Singapore in October 1998, following the decision of the Eighth Workshop in Puncak, Indonesia in December 1997. The Singapore Meeting agreed to recommend to the Ninth Workshop in 1998 that a GEM (Group of Experts Meeting) on SAR and Unlawful Acts at Sea be established and convened to discuss, among others, the issues enumerated in the Second TWG-SNSC. The Singapore Meeting noted the existence of the trilateral agreement between Indonesia, Malaysia and Singapore to eradicate piracy and armed robbery as well as illegal acts at sea in the southwest part of the South China Sea. It also noted that this effort has significantly reduced illegal acts in that area at least before the economic crisis in East Asia. The Meeting requested the participants from the three countries to prepare a briefing note on the modalities of the arrangements so that the workshop participants could consider the possibility of developing similar arrangements in other parts of the South China Sea. The Meeting also considered establishing contact with the IMB-RPC office in Kuala Lumpur. The Singapore Meeting also recommended to the Ninth Workshop that two meetings be convened in 1999 on this matter, namely the Third Meeting of the GEM-Hydrographic Data and Information Exchange (HDI) and the GEM on SAR and Unlawful Acts at Sea.

The Ninth Workshop in Ancol, Jakarta, in December 1998 approved the recommendation. The GEM on SAR and Unlawful Acts at Sea was held in Kota Kinabalu, Sabah, Malaysia in June 1999. In this Meeting, the topics enumerated in the previous TWG-SNSC were further discussed with a view to looking for and devising co-operative efforts in those fields in the South China Sea. In addition, it was hoped that Indonesia, Malaysia and Singapore could brief the meeting on the tripartite arrangement against illegal acts at sea in the Straits of Malacca and Singapore, as well as on the outcome of contact and networking with the IMB-RPC office in Kuala Lumpur.

The First Meeting of the Group of Experts on SAR and Illegal Acts at Sea in the South China Sea at Kota Kinabalu, Sabah:

1. urged relevant Authorities around the South China Sea to become party to the relevant IMO Conventions, particularly the 1976 International Convention on Maritime Search and Rescue and the 1988 Convention for the Suppression of Unlawful Acts Against the Safety of Maritime Navigation (SUA Convention);

2. encouraged relevant authorities to take measures to implement the provisions of the UNCLOS 1982 regarding SAR and Illegal Acts at Sea, particularly Article 98 on SAR, Articles 100,105,107 and 110 on Piracy; Article 108 on Illicit Trafficking in Drugs; and Article 99 on the prohibition of the transportation of slaves;

3. encouraged relevant Authorities to identify clearly their enforcement agencies at the local level for reporting acts of piracy and other illegal acts at sea, with a view to expediting and facilitating measures against illegal acts at sea;

4. recommended that the Fourth Technical Working Group on Legal Matters examine the Draft Regional Agreement on Co-operation in Combating Acts of Piracy and Armed Robbery Against Ships, contained in Annex 5 of the Report of the IMO Regional Seminar and Workshop on Piracy and Armed Robbery Against Ships, held in Singapore in February 1999, and consider its relevance to the South China Sea region;

5. requested the South China Sea Informal Working Group (SCS-IWG) in Vancouver and the Center for Southeast Asian Studies in Jakarta to obtain more information with regard to illegal acts at sea from the IMO and the IMB, and circulate it to all participants;

6. recommended to the Tenth Workshop on Managing Potential Conflicts in the South China Sea that the Second Meeting of the Group of Experts on SAR and Illegal Acts at Sea be convened in 2000 to assess the progress achieved on the above recommendations and to discuss further means to promote co-operation on this matter.

The Fourth Meeting of the Technical Working Group on Legal Matters in the South China Sea, held in Koh Samui, Thailand, 27–28 September 1999, discussed the Recommendations of the First Meeting of the Group of

Experts on SAR as requested and agreed to recommend to the Eleventh Workshop that "a Group of Legal and Technical Experts be convened to examine the ASEAN-SAR Agreements, the IMO 1999 SAR Convention, the pertinent provisions of the UN Convention on the Law of the Sea, 1982, and Annex 5 of the Report of the IMO Regional Seminar and Workshop on Piracy and Armed Robbery Against Ships, held in Singapore in February 1999, and to consider their relevance to the South China Sea region".

The Tenth Workshop in Bogor, 5–8 December 1999 discussed and endorsed the reports and recommendations of the Kinabalu Meeting and agreed to give priority to the GEM on SAR and Illegal Acts at Sea to deal with the problems of combating piracy and armed robbery against ships, and enhancing SAR arrangements in the South China Sea region. In fact, the Tenth Workshop agreed that the Second Meeting of the GEM on SAR and Illegal Acts at Sea on the suppression of piracy and armed robbery at sea and SAR be held in 2000. Unfortunately, however, due to budgetary problems and the pressure of activities of the Second Meeting of the GEM on SAR and Illegal Acts at Sea as well as the Group of Legal and Technical Experts to examine the existing Conventions as requested by the Fourth TWG-LM in Koh Samui, this meeting has not yet been convened.

Conclusions

Any effort to intensify law enforcement, whether on land or at sea, would have to consider several factors.

1. Conflicting regulations are very common in some countries making it difficult for law enforcement agencies to implement them. The law itself must be clear and should not give rise to conflicting interpretations, and laws regarding various maritime issues should not be contradictory.

2. The law enforcement agencies and officials must have sufficient and thorough knowledge of the laws and regulations which they have to enforce and all of them must be free of corruption and graft. Otherwise no matter how clear the law is, law enforcement activities will not be successful.

3. There must be a clear line of command and responsibility in the law enforcement agencies so that accountability is clear. Under the Indonesian legal system, apparently inherited from the old Dutch legal system, a public prosecutor may "shelve" ("deponer" in Dutch), a case if he thinks its continuation may negatively affect public interest. In some cases, this could lead to corruption.

4. If in certain countries, the law enforcement activities involve several agencies, the division of authority and the co-ordination of activities must be clearly outlined and well understood by the respective agencies so that there will not be overlapping jurisdiction in certain cases or denial of jurisdiction in other cases. This is a problem with *Bakorkamla*, particularly since the agency was only supposed to co-ordinate and lacked enforcement authority and capacity. Moreover, interagency rivalries are frequent and counterproductive.

5. As in many other governmental activities, effective law enforcement activities, including those at sea with regard to piracy and other illegal acts, depend to a great extent on the availability of the 5Ms, namely Men, Money, Materials, Methodology, and Management. If one of these is missing, then law enforcement will be difficult. In fact, all of these "M's" are lacking in Indonesia and many other developing countries, particularly for fighting crime at sea.

6. The support of the people is also essential in implementing any law or regulation. If the law or regulation is contrary to common sense or a general sense of justice and appropriateness, it will be difficult to implement, even if the law enforcement agencies are strong. Indeed the Government and the law enforcement agencies could be regarded as "dictatorial" or "totalitarian" by the common people if the laws and regulations do not reflect a sense of justice or appropriateness.

7. The laws and regulations to be implemented should not be against the spirit of good neighbourly relations and should observe the rules of international law, including the law of the sea. The law enforcement agencies should also therefore understand and take into account the rules of international law and the various regional and international conventions applicable or dealing with those particular issues. Otherwise the rules and regulations to be enforced could be challenged by other states.

The challenges in developing co-operative security and enforcement policy regarding piracy in Southeast Asia include the following:

1. The ability of national governments to make a timely and sustained response to the perpetrators of piracy and armed robbery at sea must be promoted and strengthened. Due to the current economic crisis in Southeast Asia, particularly in Indonesia, the need for support for Indonesian law enforcement agencies to strengthen their capabilities is paramount. This support could be regional or international or from countries which have a direct and specific interest in the matter. The increasing possibility of maritime crimes and international terrorism in Southeast Asian waters should stimulate such support for coastal countries as well as regional co-operation.

2. The promotion of border co-operation between and among neighbouring countries is also very important. The efforts to promote solutions and agreements on maritime boundary delimitation between and among Southeast Asian countries should be intensified so that the activities and the area of operation of the various national law enforcement agencies, as well as that for bilateral and regional co-operation, could be clarified.

3. Various efforts at the regional level, either formal or informal to promote regional understanding and co-operation in this area should be supported. The draft of a Regional Agreement on Co-operation in Combating Acts of Piracy and Armed Robbery Against Ships, formulated under IMO auspices, should be studied and finalized as soon as possible in a manner that is acceptable to the countries in Southeast Asia and the South China Sea. Informally, the initiatives and activities of the South China Sea Workshop process, particularly the activities and work of its Group of Experts on Illegal Acts at Sea should be supported. For ten years (1990–2000), the South China Sea Workshop process was supported by Canada through the University of British Columbia in Vancouver and the Center for South East Asian Studies in Jakarta. Now that support has terminated. The South China Sea Workshop process is therefore encountering difficulties in continuing its management of potential conflicts in the South China Sea through dialogue, confidence-building, and promotion of co-operative efforts. These

efforts have been lauded worldwide as a constructive informal mechanism in the area and it is hoped that continued support for the process will be forthcoming.

4. Finally, within the context of implementing Articles 43 and 100 of the 1982 UNCLOS regarding the obligation of all states "to co-operate to the fullest extent in the repression of piracy", the coastal states of Southeast Asia and the South China Sea should co-operate with the user states and the relevant regional and international organizations, such as IMO, to formulate and undertake anti-piracy policies and activities, and the European states should extend their support to this effort.

8

Conclusion:
Towards an Agenda for
Piracy Research

Derek Johnson and Mark Valencia

The chapters in this volume were written by a cross-section of academics trying to better understand piracy and thus to formulate effective responses to it. The main themes that emerge in the volume dominate contemporary discussions of piracy and counter-pirate activities in Southeast Asia. These themes can be clustered into two broad categories: the characteristics of piracy in Southeast Asia, and measures to control piracy in the region.

Considerable attention in the volume was devoted to the definition and quantification of piracy, two issues of central importance to piracy in Southeast Asia and, indeed, in all piracy prone regions of the world. The definitional issue remains an important point of discussion not the least because the two major international organizations responsible for counter piracy initiatives, the IMO and the IMB, have significantly different approaches to the definition of piracy. The IMO has opted for a relatively comprehensive definition that distinguishes between piracy and armed robbery at sea, while the IMB employs a much more open-ended definition.

The contributors to this volume raise numerous issues of relevance to the definition of piracy. Of these, two are particularly worth highlighting. First, none adhere strictly to the terminological distinction upheld by the IMO, although the importance of the distinction between pirate acts committed in international waters and in national waters is underscored as foundational to the co-ordination difficulties between states in Southeast Asia for counter piracy efforts. The geographical boundaries imposed by the 1982 UNCLOS are thus of major importance for understanding constraints on responses to piracy.

Second, while there is general acknowledgement that piracy takes many forms, from petty theft to co-ordinated hijacking, there are divergent emphases in some articles between what might be labelled as inclusive and particularistic approaches to defining piracy. Ong advocates the inclusive position, arguing that it is advisable to conflate piracy with terrorism in order to stimulate co-ordinated action by Southeast Asian states on regional security. But Valencia explicitly questions Ong's conflation hypothesis, arguing for the utility of retaining the distinction between piracy and terrorism. In doing so, he shares with Young and Chaikin emphasis on the diversity or, in Chaikin's terms, multidimensionality of piracy. Their approaches are particularistic in that they highlight the historical and geographical conditions that shape piracy. Young in particular shows clearly how definitions of piracy themselves are products of particular political circumstances, such as colonialism.

The historical perspective also helps to contextualise the intensity of pirate attacks. Young shows, for example, how conditions in the mid-nineteenth century contributed to a steep rise in piracy while reduced naval presence after end of the Cold War may have also led to growth in piracy. Similarly, the recent growth in the frequency and violence of pirate attacks in Southeast Asia can be attributed to the changed political conditions and economic instability.

Reference to a particularistic approach to piracy that results from attention to piracy's context, leads to discussion of this volume's second theme: strategies for the suppression of piracy in Southeast Asia. Here three general approaches may be discerned: use of defensive technologies like ShipLoc; the deepening of internationally co-ordinated strategies for piracy suppression; and regional development to provide alternatives for pirate recruits. The first two approaches are accepted as important by all authors in the book but only Young, Valencia, and Djalal argue for the importance of regional development. That Young and Valencia should advocate regional development is not a surprise, given the attention that they draw to economic marginality as a contributor to poverty. Young makes the interesting proposal that shipping companies threatened by piracy might become sources of funding for coastal development initiatives in piracy prone areas if such efforts would be seen to make an impact on the prevalence of piracy. Djalal's advocacy of increased assistance to Indonesia for development of anti-piracy measures is also not surprising, given the serious poverty of the country and its apparent inability to suppress piracy within its waters.

Considerable attention in this volume is focussed on the challenges of regional co-operation. The strong option for regional co-operation is SUA, which is favoured by Singapore, the US, and India, but which is viewed suspiciously by Indonesia and some other Southeast Asian countries which see it as undermining their sovereignty. The conflation of piracy with terrorism proposed by Ong might serve to nudge these countries towards signing SUA. The more likely avenue for progress is the slow building of an international regime through Track Two dialogue. The recent initiatives by Japan in the areas of joint coast guard patrols and capacity building are promising in this regard, particularly as they match the political interests of the most sensitive state for security in the region — Indonesia. The widespread awareness among policymakers in the region of the threat of terrorists using the tactics of pirates may stimulate the hastening of informal connections, even if it does not result in formal accession to treaties like SUA.

Building Blocks in an Agenda for Piracy Research

In the Southeast Asian context where the incidence and violence of piracy has been growing and where maritime terrorism is a threat with potentially horrific consequences, there is an urgent need to come up with innovate ways to counter maritime violence. This volume has provided the empirical foundation for that effort and has proposed some important starting points for policy formulation.

The immediate practical challenge that emerges clearly from the contributions to this book is the need to continue to support initiatives to build trust and co-operation at the regional level in Southeast Asia. This area should remain a major focus for research along with continued close monitoring of the incidence of piracy. Key research questions regarding the geopolitics of piracy and piracy prevention are the following:

- Why is it so difficult to forge co-operation in suppressing piracy?
- How does piracy affect international relations and how do international relations affect responses to piracy?
- Which, if any, nation's leadership in an anti-piracy effort might be acceptable in the region?
- What is politically acceptable for the United States? What is the appropriate role of other Asian countries like China, Japan, and India?
- How can the geopolitical issues be circumvented or downplayed in order to get governments to respond to piracy more effectively? Specifically, how can Southeast Asian countries best be encouraged to co-operate to suppress piracy without allowing sovereignty issues to intervene?
- What are appropriate short-term responses and long-term strategies? What are their respective costs and benefits?

The second research challenge raised in this volume is the conflation of piracy and terrorism, which can be operationalized as follows:

- Is there an evolving relationship between piracy and terrorism?
- Is this real, imagined, possible, or probable?
- What are the advantages and disadvantages of conflating piracy and terrorism in terms of stimulating political co-operation, and in terms of legal and physical responses?

Despite the richness of these areas of enquiry, the study of contemporary piracy remains a relatively narrow field. Much less attention has been paid to a number of other topics, some of which may have direct utility for combating piracy. Perhaps most importantly, as Young has indicated, researchers have neglected the social and economic contexts that give rise to piracy. At present, counter-piracy measures are primarily reactive and superficial in their emphasis on the suppression of piracy and on its deterrence through physical measures. Research on the contexts and causes of piracy could result in the development of preventative measures to control piracy that would complement ongoing work on reactive measures.

Some work in this area has already been undertaken. Piracy has been equated with banditry, which increases during times of economic and political uncertainty. In such circumstances local authorities may be unwilling to, uninterested in, or unable to enforce counter-piracy laws. Inability may be due to economic limitations, such as the lack of funds to buy coastguard vessels for surveillance. In other situations, corruption may undermine law enforcement and the courts, or chronic ethnic conflict may make intervention risky even for state military forces. It has even been argued that clandestine activities may be more culturally acceptable in some areas, such as Malaysia and Indonesia where there is a long tradition of depredation, robbery, and smuggling during times when fishing is unremunerative. It is also important to pay attention to seemingly minor contextual changes, like shrinking crew sizes due to technological innovation, which has made ships more vulnerable to attack. As Valencia notes, a small but important segment of groups involved in piracy is connected to international crime syndicates but the extent and manner of their involvement in piracy is poorly understood. It would be useful to establish who belong to these organizations, what their structure is, how they operate, and how they are linked to other forms of organized crime.

This area could be labelled as the criminology of piracy, and the research agenda of the following questions could be grounded in:

- What are the context and causes of piracy?
- Who are pirates?
- What are their motives?
- What are the socio-cultural and economic environments within which they are operating?
- Are some "high end" pirates linked to other illegal activities such as smuggling, kidnapping, black marketeering, or poaching?
- What is the role of corruption both in enforcement and perpetration?
- Are some pirates simply unemployed fishermen and, if so, why are they unemployed?
- How do pirates react to attempts to control their activities?
- What specific kinds of regional development are required and what are their costs and benefits? Are there stakeholder groups like ship owners who might be willing to fund such initiatives?

All of these enquiries into the criminology of piracy raise an important methodological question. What data gathering strategies are appropriate to studying a topic with such great political sensitivity and where the primary data-gathering methods of social science are difficult or impossible?

Relatively little is known about the economics of piracy, which would be another area of value for piracy studies and might address questions such as the following:

- What is the impact of piracy on shipping and trade?
- What are the actual costs of piracy, both measurable and intangible?
- What are the costs of alternative counter piracy initiatives?
- Are the costs of responses justified by the costs of piracy?
- Are the costs of "policing" the oceans a major problem, or is piracy more a problem of international relations than of actual costs?

Finally, a topic of more purely academic interest anticipated by Young is the transformation of piracy of the meaning of piracy over time. Reformulated as a research question; how is piracy and piracy suppression represented in official and media documents? What interests predominate and which are absent from such representations? We believe these questions provide an agenda for research, which can enhance understanding of the phenomenon of piracy and aid the formulation of effective responses to it.

Index